NORTHUMBERLAND

A CELEBRATION

NORTHUMBERLAND

A CELEBRATION

STAN BECKENSALL

FONTHILL

Fonthill Media Limited
www.fonthillmedia.com
office@fonthillmedia.com

First published in the United Kingdom 2015

British Library Cataloguing in Publication Data:
A catalogue record for this book is available from the British Library

ISBN 978-1-78155-253-7

Typeset in 10.5pt on 13pt Sabon
Printed and bound in England

Contents

Preface

This book is a celebration of some of the things that are of enduring interest to me in Northumberland. Although I have been writing about archaeology and landscape since the 1970s, I wrote *The Power of Place* in 2001, prefaced then by these words:

> Places generate feelings; some do this because we have learnt what happened there, some because they are physically striking or beautiful, and others because they have some indefinable attraction and quality.

The same applies today, and I have added more places to my discoveries. I also still maintain an approach that is not chronological. It is grounded in fact; but I have also included some poetry when only this can describe the indescribable. I join with my artist friends who use other media to express their reaction to places that are included.

This approach has to be selective, and I hope that the omission of places and events that many readers cherish will not cause regret. With the increased interest in the county, through visitors and through easier access to many places such as castles and the Roman Wall trail in the media and advertising, I have not concentrated solely on the best-known places, as the county is full of sites that say much about the way people have lived here or still do.

Acknowledgements

I am grateful to so many people who have shared their knowledge with me, especially the late Anna Rossiter, Peter Ryder, Peter Carne, Paul Frodsham, and Hugh Dixon. I am grateful to those who have read the text in pre-publication phases over many years, particularly to Matthew Hutchinson. Stephen Hope initially helped me with his computer skills from the outset and has taken great interest in the content.

Maps are by Richard Parkin, Marc Johnstone and Paul Brown.

The photographs are my own, except that by Tony Illey, otherwise stated. My thanks to the University of Newcastle.

The artwork of Birtley Aris and Gordon Highmore shares my interest in landscape, buildings, and atmosphere.

Introduction

Important events in Northumberland continue to add to people's awareness of the many things that this county has to offer. For example, the *Lindisfarne Gospels* have been returned for a while to Durham from London, and attract huge audiences. What we now call Holy Island is where they were written, and they represent the so-called Golden Age of Northumbria when Christianity was rooted here and spread widely through the writing of the four Gospels and their embellishment as an art form worthy of their subject matter.

There is a plan to build a new National Park tourist centre south of Hadrian's Wall to serve the Wall corridor at Twice Brewed. Although this is not to everyone's taste, it will help parties of pupils who find themselves soaked sometimes by heavy rain to find refuge after their exertions. Such refuges are also provided by the Vindolanda Trust at its two centres.

The 500th Anniversary of the Battle of Flodden took place in 2013, a battle in which so many English and Scots were slaughtered in the last major battle between the two nations, fought on the often-lawless land on the Border. This is hardly a matter for celebration, though, but rather another example of how power politics destroy ordinary people.

Hexham Abbey has been reunited with its claustral buildings, part of which were re-cycled after the Dissolution of the Monasteries, to be a home for important local families, a courthouse and social service offices. Now, with great skill and expense, there is a great new development that has become a centre for telling the story of the development of the whole Abbey complex and a place for talks, musical performances, and other meetings, as befits Hexham's finest building.

Research into Northumberland's past continues to flourish through documents and through archaeology, and the involvement of people who wish to be trained in research techniques. The latest archaeology group, the Tynedale Archaeology group, is examining the area north of the Wall, and recording significant discoveries with the help of professional archaeological surveyors. Meanwhile sites like Vindolanda offer top-class excavation, research and display, with the addition of the remarkable Vindolanda writing tablets on view in a carefully-controlled setting.

There is so much more to come in the discovery of the past, for Northumberland still has more of its story to tell in superb settings. Its industrial past is part of this, and the investigation of such things as lead-mining sites grows yearly. And so many people are given the chance to be involved.

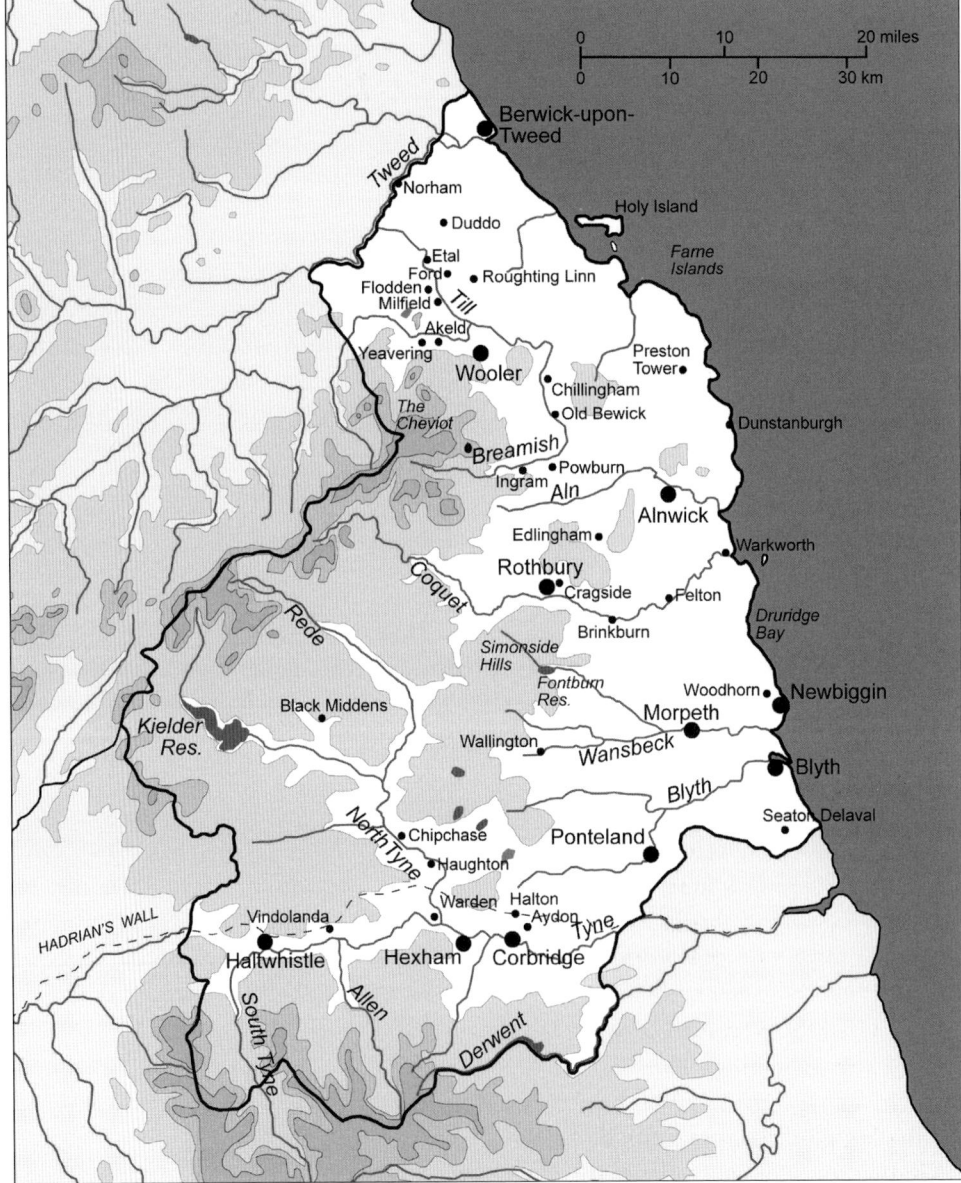

The map shows some of the places mentioned in the text, and is intended as a base for the use of more detailed maps published by Ordnance Survey, especially the Pathfinder series. (*Marc Johnstone*)

Above and Below the Surface: Old Bewick

POEMS OF THE MOORLAND

1. Sunset: Old Bewick

Autumn sun westering;
Fire in amber floods this land.
A distant kestrel floats on air
That draws the eye from gold to violet.
Rocks on hillsides spring to life,
Sheep whiten in encrusted bracken
Where ruts run like inked lines.
Ramparts on hill forts
Raise themselves to catch the fading light,
Their ditches subterranean, black as jet.
Beyond the scarp, the shredded clouds have gathered,
Radiating sunlight, myriads of beams
That roll fields and streams along,
Awakening the river snake
And raking woods with light.
Rough moorland throbs against pale pasture,
Meets mosaics on stone walls:
A life beyond a life: one calm and smooth,
One rifted, broken up and full of mystery.
And at this meeting place
A tilted table rock, absorbing light,
Libating gold from man-made grooves;
Fluidity, concentric circles leaping into life
And fading with the sun-slip down the scarp.
Black rooks erupt above stiff Douglas fir,
Blown fragments from a fire

That drift awhile, and rest.
Like giant wings, the shadows of the night
Beat out the light.
Blawearie house absorbs a depth of red
That hovers the warm air
Before magenta in the sky cries welcome to the stars.

2. Moonlight

Scattered stagnant ponds
Like silver hoof-prints
Diffuse moonlight,
Image intermittent cloud.
Marsh grass shatters, ice-like,
Furze holds bobbing shreds of wool
Plucked from sheep whose coiled horns
Bow to whispers of stained teeth and tongues.
Round-backed boulders stroked with shadow
Hold earth-fast.
Wheel ruts running deeper fade into a far horizon,
Stretching out the moorland to a mystery
In which a sudden fluttering of wings
Or startled cry from sluggish burn or blackened copse
Echoes from a rock-torn clough.
Moonlight lies like frost upon a heather-crusted knoll.
Owl hovers, lands on hawthorn bush,
Grey on spiky black.

OLD BEWICK MOOR

Northumberland has many spectacular viewpoints; the west-facing scarp on the edge of Old Bewick Moor is one of them. In bright summer sunshine, in mist, snow or rain, perspectives change. Heather blooms, bracken dies, cloudscapes regroup frequently and quickly. For many, the rolling hills and valleys and the places from which we view them are so attractive that they are sufficient in themselves for our enjoyment. Awareness of what forces have shaped such landscapes does not detract from aesthetic enjoyment; it can add considerably to our interest in it. We can find intensity in a grain of sand; we can become aware of the natural power that has shaped our landscape, so that each addition to our knowledge increases our aware-ness of the layers of time and meaning. We then build on this. The Cheviot Hills that rise above the Breamish–Till valley to the west lie at the heart of the region. Almost 400 million years ago they were formed by great volcanic upheavals, with ash exploding into the air and lava flowing over the land. The process lasted for millions of years and the results were diverse; differences in rock types within this mass are not easy to discern from such a distance

The scarp is made of different material, the result of sedimentary sands, muds, and shells being deposited thousands of metres thick in the Carboniferous period, with the Fell sandstone, as it is called, at Old Bewick being made entirely out of sand. This scarp is of great historic importance; one can see the way it runs from north to south, then gently swings to continue from Alnwick to Rothbury, where it forms the distinctive block of the Simonside Hills. The middle courses of the Rivers Aln and Breamish can be seen from here.

To the north-east, as we turn our backs on the Cheviots, the dip slope gently leads us over moorland broken up by occasional quarries for sand, stone, coal and limestone, towards the coastal plain. To the west is the unique double enclosure on the edge of the scarp; in the other direction *Ros Castle*, with its pre-Roman earthworks of ditches and walls, is a splendid place from which to view the continuation of this apparently deserted landscape to the more fertile areas along the coast. The same is true of the Old Bewick 'hill fort'.

Ice sheets have swept across the region to scour the rocks and to lay down fresh deposits such as boulder clay. South of Powburn the meltwater cuts deep channels into rock. As we look across the valley from the scarp to the Cheviots we see beyond the tilted sandstones the deposits of glacial material, and on the moors behind we find broken and smoothed erratics among walls and other stone piles. A brief look at the stones of the Blawearie cairns reveals a good mixture of sandstones, some with fossils, and igneous fragments.

The Old Bewick landscape is more 'angular' than the rounded Cheviots, and is mostly heather-covered, except where there has been deliberate clearing of the heather and planting of grass. The contrast between heather moorland and pasture is striking on Old Bewick Moor. The Harehope Burn cuts a valley through near-horizontal layers of sandstone, forming some steep cliffs, like those at *Corby Crag*, and huge blocks of sandstone outcrop dramatically at Blawearie house. The rise and fall of the land further east does not lead us uniformly to the sea, but provides enough variation in contour to please the eye, despite the uniformity of vegetation.

Farms, houses and other buildings have been rare on these moors, and are now mostly deserted and decayed. The more fertile and accessible lands that lie at the scarp foot and beyond are where people chose to live and work. From the scarp, the modern farm of New Bewick, with its arable fields, small woods and pigsties forms a discrete unit of farm buildings and houses. It lies close to the A697 road and the site of the Battle of Hedgeley Moor, commemorated by a walled display at the roadside.

What the eye does not always see is that under the soil are monuments and settlements revealed by parchmarks in the ploughsoil where the sites of prehistoric cairns, enclosed farms and Saxon houses lie. Nearby, the Roman road, the Devil's Causeway, runs from Hadrian's Wall to Scotland.

Parts of Old Bewick village have gone; a road from Alnwick to Chatton runs over a demolished but documented fortified tower. The name of the small cluster

A view from Old Bewick scarp west across the Breamish/Till valley to the Cheviot Hills.

Ros castle: a prehistoric enclosure.

Old Bewick village from the scarp: the village school is on the right.

of houses is from Old English, meaning the bee farm, presumably famous for its honey. Other villages and towns, such as Berwick (barley farm), Cheswick (cheese farm) and Goswick (where the geese are) also lay claim to specialised products. Beal, close to the causeway to Holy Island, is the hill of bees. Today the settlement ribbons along the road, beginning at the south with a modern 'underground' house that retains an old wall round it, past a water mill now used as a farm store. There is a redundant school with the Baker-Cresswell squirrel emblem denoting its origin. Strangely, the church is tucked away in the Kirk (church) Burn valley with no signs of any houses nearby. Outside the church a massive sandstone slab spans the burn to carry a footpath to Blawearie.

For some, the village of sandstone is only the starting point for the trek up to Old Bewick Moor, but it has a significant place in history. John Charles Langlands, from a family of well-known silversmiths and goldsmiths in Newcastle, brought his family to set up home here in the nineteenth century, choosing to live the life of a country squire, to the great advantage of this community. His family shared his involvement; his daughters are named in the school logbook helping to teach children. He received accolades, with other enlightened Northumberland farmers, from Agricultural Commissions for establishing the decent accommodation for his farm workers that can be seen today. At a time when the Annual Hirings (when workers hired themselves and their families out to a farmer for a year's work) were commonplace, his own workers had little desire to leave him. He kept his shepherds for years, and trained his own farm managers.

When he arrived, Old Bewick church was a ruin, but he joined others enthusiastically in its restoration. As we shall see, he had the good taste to save the interior from plaster and whitewash, leaving beautiful bare stone. His service is marked by a cross dedicated to him at the end of the lane to the church; plaques in the building commemorate him and some of his children.

PREHISTORIC ROCK ART

The work of one man can be seen in the small community, but I have another particular reason to revere his memory. When I first came to Northumberland in late 1966 I visited Old Bewick Moor, where a large block of sandstone lies on the hillslope, dumped there by ice. It interested John Langlands, who speculated on the origin and meaning of the cup and ring marks that decorate its surface.

> J. C. Langlands discovered some worn and defaced figures incised on a rude sandstone block, near to the great camp on Old Bewick Hill in north Northumberland. Though strange and old-world looking, these figures then presented an isolated fact, and he hesitated to connect them with by-past ages; for they might have been the recent work of an ingenious shepherd, while resting on a hill; but on finding, some years afterwards, another incised stone of a similar character on the same hill, he then formed the opinion, that these sculptures were very ancient. To him belongs the honour of the first discovery of these archaic sculptures. . .

Thus wrote George Tate, the Alnwick historian, of the discovery of the first what we call rock art in the 1820s.

The place has a special power and significance, for here my own curiosity, already aroused in Malta by the spirals and tendrils on Megalithic temples, led me to years of part-time work to learn more about the origin, use and meaning of the symbols.

Even without its motifs the rock is impressive. Perhaps five thousand years ago it attracted people to cover its surface with motifs pecked with a hard stone tool, impacted with a mallet. Nearby are others, mostly on near-horizontal slabs, that attracted an interest that was hardly utilitarian. The rock is at a prominent viewpoint, and the design of 'cups and rings' with linear grooves is common throughout Britain and in some places abroad, such as Galicia; occasionally they are found in burial mounds, on standing stones and in rock shelters. Here the serious study of rock art began. It led me to record every panel in Northumberland and many other parts of Britain as a leisure-time activity. It is both satisfying and frustrating: more data does not necessarily lead to the answers we seek. Much of the mystery remains, and that has its own fascination.

The late Ronald Morris, a distinguished Scottish solicitor, was moved by great curiosity to explore in detail not only sites in Britain where rock art occurs but all over the world. He spent much of his retirement seeking answers to questions that we still ask. He and I were aware of the difficulty of trying to explain something

Old Bewick rock in its setting, with Hepburn in the background.

Cup and ring motifs on the
rock surface. (*Birtley Aris*)

that meant so much to people living over five thousand years ago. Unlike pictures of people or animals, abstract symbols hide layers of meaning. Will the discovery of crosses in the distant future enable archaeologists to understand what they mean to Christians? We absorb symbols into many aspects of our lives: road signs, washing machine symbols, car logos, the National Park curlew are but a few. We take them for granted and know what they represent because we grow up with them. What then can we make of symbols devised by people deep in the past? We try to use our experience to interpret them, and project ourselves into them in such a way that their meaning may become what we want it to be.

One of Ronald's contributions to the study was his teasing out 104 explanations gleaned from many sources to account for these symbols, and he gave the explanations marks out of ten for their credibility. He was strongly convinced that they had a religious and magical significance, as their presence in burials and on standing stones suggested. He was not at all happy with the idea that they denoted breasts, the Mother Goddess, eyes and phallic symbols, or that they were connected with fertility rites. He rated some theories with a zero: copies of worm casts, messages from outer space, places where adders regularly curled up to sleep, doodles and games, for example. One popular and unsupported theory suggested that they were maps. There was an amusing comment made at a lecture in which the speaker was convinced that they were maps of Iron Age hill forts. As we know that the marks were made hundreds of years before the hill forts were built, a lady in the audience said that she had heard of retrospective planning permission, but that was ridiculous! When we come face to face with an apparently insoluble problem such as why people made these marks all over the world, we are bound to let our minds go free and speculate about their origin, use and meaning. I have done the same thing, as this poem written in 1974 shows:

The Sculptured Rocks

In this design you petrified the language of your soul—
Your own symbolic logic;
Linked a little world with universe,
Arrested time with space.
You saw the cycle of your birth and death with clarity
As sun and moon spun round,
As buds burst into leaves and fell upon the nourished ground.
A rhythmic pulse beat out like water flow,
Rippled from your centre to the stars.
The living rocks bear traces of belief,
Knowing all you used to know.
The curlew cry spills out
A plaintive, bubbling message to the moors
Above the desecrated graves and broken stones
As it has always done.

Its curved beak swings down from the sun
To execute parabolas in heather-scented air,
Or sink in silence to an unresponsive earth.

    Our response to rock art is influenced by places where it is situated and our instinctive reactions when we view it. The more we know about it, though, the less certain we become; all our knowledge brings us nearer to our ignorance. We try to understand it from its context; in the landscape it appears on some outcrop and earthfast rocks that are either at prominent viewpoints or at special places such as spring sources. They 'sign the land' for the people who moved through it. Later the meaning changed from the open-air when the symbols were buried with the dead, not intended to be seen. They were pecked onto some standing stones, suggesting a role in ritual. Yet they are only in a very small number of burials and on few monuments. It is possible that the marks could also have been made on perishable material such as wood, cloth or human skin.

    The motifs may be evidence of the earliest human activity on this moor, although it is possible that earlier hunter-gatherers made use of paths in their pursuit of game and other food. There followed a more settled way of life for some when the lower lands were cultivated, fences erected and circular houses built of wood and thatch. Animals were domesticated, and probably brought to the uplands in summer for grazing, thus remaining an important source of food that was supplemented by hunting. The vegetation on this scarpland would have been different from today's. The soil is thin and poor, acidic, and would have supported light woodland. What we see is the result of centuries of different use; it is from snippets of documents and from rare analysis of buried soils that we can form some idea of such changes.

    It is largely in Northumberland that our knowledge of the extent of prehistoric rock-art has developed nationally, and today much of the research on this bewildering phenomenon is based. Following the discovery of well over 1,000 different pieces of rock art on outcrop, boulders, portable stones, material in burial cairns, on rock-shelters and standing stones, the archive produced by the author was taken into Newcastle University, put onto their website, and this currently has resulted in 17 million hits on the Internet. However, the main significance of work is that it has attracted others to work on the subject, at universities and by anyone who finds in it good reason to explore places themselves, which gives them an added interest in the county and in all parts of the world where rock art is represented. Many have come from abroad to study what we have here.

The Northumberland website itself was given The Channel 4 Television British Archaeological Award for 2006 in the ICT category Winner to Dr Aron Mazel , ICCHS, University of Newcastle and to Dr Stan Beckensall. It is known as Northumberland Rock Art: Access to the Beckensall Archive.

    So far no settlements earlier than the hill forts have been found on Old Bewick Moor, but on Hepburn Moor, which lies to the north, two sites of prehistoric settlement have been identified. Other activity is well-marked by a number of burial mounds, some with the cists visible at the centre. They are high in the landscape.

A panel of rock art outcrop outside the hill enclosure.

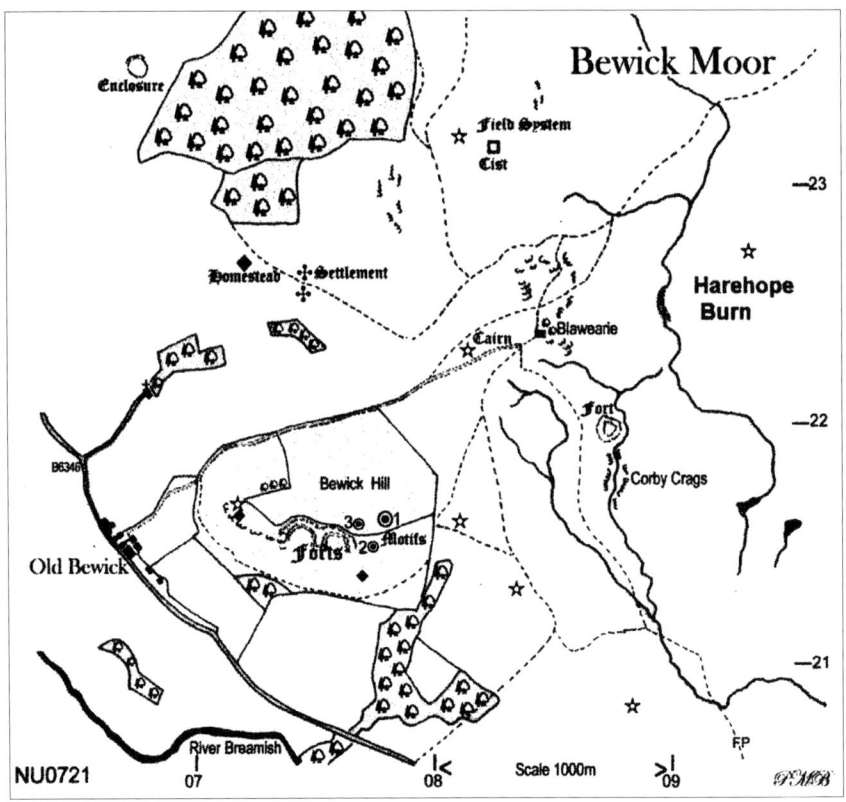

Location of sites in this part of the text. (*Paul Brown*)

The name *Hepburn* means 'the high burial mounds'. Burials have attracted the curious and the greedy, as depressions at the centre of some cairns indicate. Some may for a while have been protected by legends and the fear of what might happen if the dead were disturbed. We know that some have been 'explored' in recent times without any records being made, and some have been used to bury dead sheep.

The mounds are piles of stone that cover a body, a cremation, often in a pit, or an inhumation or cremation in a cist, a stone-lined box with a capstone to seal it. 'Cist' means a chest and in local mines the Deputy kept his records in a cist. In Scotland one kind of cist contains clothing and other material stored for a wedding day.

Small pieces of worked flint that have been found in the area may be connected to hunting activity, although some, like pieces of jet and shale that are 'collected' from the moors may be from burial cairns.

A cist, from which the burial on Hepburn hill was taken many years ago. (*Birtley Aris*)

THE BLAWEARIE CAIRNS

The most important early Bronze Age burial site on the moor is known as the Blawearie Cairns. The large and small cairns have been excavated; the story they tell is fascinating. Here the power of place can be felt as well as seen, for the cairns occupy a position in the landscape on one of two rounded deposits of glacial sands that have extensive views. They are in a kind of wide amphitheatre, overlooked by higher ground from which they can easily be seen. Today the largest of the mounds, about 40 feet (12 m) in diameter, has been restored/reinstated to allow visitors to understand the story of its building and use. Other smaller Early Bronze Age cairns cluster around it, some excavated and others not, all dating from around 2000 BC. This is a prehistoric cemetery.

Like many other mounds in Northumberland, the largest was dug into in the nineteenth century by Canon William Greenwell, a canon of Durham cathedral who spent much of his long life excavating and fishing (the 'Greenwell fly' is well-known to fishermen). His influence as a digger and recorder was extensive; he amassed a collection of artefacts that is now deposited in the British Museum, and wrote copiously. His report on the Blawearie cairn is rather brief and could have been more helpful. He dug the mound, first noting in the centre a pit that had been dug by persons unknown, and that it had contained a possible cist burial and some pottery. He claimed then to have explored the whole interior of the mound, and found three cist graves, one with a 'food vessel', another with a jet and shale necklace and broken flint knife, and the third was declared empty. He produced no drawing of the site, only of the artefacts.

People's choice of sites to excavate may be governed by an affinity with the total landscape. Here in 1984 was someone's abandoned 'dig', overgrown with bracken and heather, untidy, with the centre sagging, littered with pieces of stone, yet the whole was surrounded by an incomplete but impressive ring of standing stones. I had often taken groups of children and adults there as part of a longer walk. It seemed such a pity that we knew so little about it.

There were so few prehistoric cairns on view in Northumberland that could give people some idea of what they looked like when first built. There was another reason, apart from sheer curiosity, that involved the rock art sites. I had already excavated cairns in which cup and ring marked cobbles and boulders had been deliberately incorporated as part of the ritual. There were major rock art sites nearby; here was a very large cairn which might incorporate rock art, and make another link between the motifs and ritual or religious practices.

Controls imposed on the excavation of Ancient Monuments are very rigid, but our proposals to excavate Blawearie were accepted. We are fond of saying that history is about people; true, and it can be about people today working together as a team to learn something about the past. The project was a Northumberland County Council one, involving the training of young people from local High Schools in the techniques of archaeology, no matter what their chosen main course of study. It was backed by experts in many fields, such as palaeobotanists from Durham University

One of many unexplored cairns between Blawearie house and the Harehope Burn.

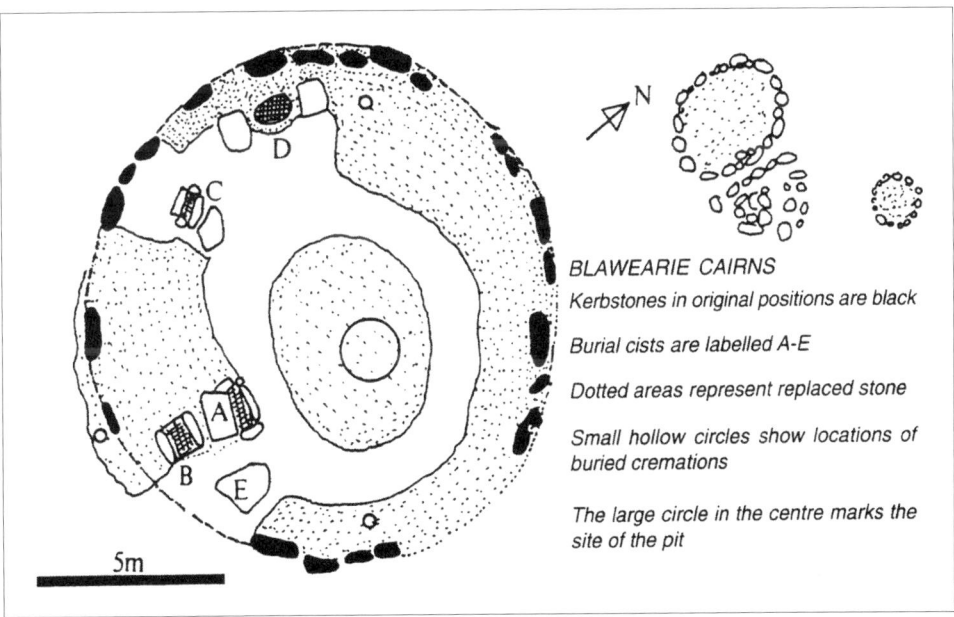

BLAWEARIE CAIRNS

Kerbstones in original positions are black

Burial cists are labelled A-E

Dotted areas represent replaced stone

Small hollow circles show locations of buried cremations

The large circle in the centre marks the site of the pit

A simplified Plan of the Blawearie excavated cairns. (*Ian Hewitt*)

and other professional archaeologists. It was inspected regularly on behalf of English Heritage. It attracted help one year from the British Conservation Volunteers, and was awarded financial help from the Shell 'Better Britain Campaign'. It was given wide media coverage. Yes, it was certainly about all kinds of people showing an interest and helping with the work.

Irene and Ian Hewitt, of Poole, whom I first met on a Ford Castle summer course, became co-Directors of the project, and Ian was mainly responsible for the final report.

An RAF air/sea rescue helicopter that trained in the area took photographs from above to add to the recording, and often landed close to the excavation, bright yellow upon the sombre vegetation. The place took on added excitement. The voices of Public School and Northumbrian mingled. 'Good grief, Prince Charles in stereo' was a local response to two of my diggers by other young people from different backgrounds.

In 1988, four years after the start of the excavation the site was complete and the cairns had been reinstated. There was no Rock Art, but the history of the mound was fairly clear. It was also discovered that around the site were smaller mounds, one containing a cremation burial in a pit. The large cairn was a focal point in a larger cemetery; the range of artefacts, human remains and structures confirmed its importance: an amber necklace, worked flint including four burnt scrapers buried with the cremated remains of a woman and child in a cist, an urn dug into the base of the mound at a later date with the burnt remains of two men. There were two other cremations, an oval 'empty' cist with two capstones, above which, and much later, a blue 'melon' bead had been inserted, perhaps by the people who built the hill fort as a votive offering.

William Greenwell had not spent long enough on the site; his trenching (which we have left traced in our reinstatement) missed so much. We concluded that there used to be a large oak tree growing where the centre of the mound is now. Its root cavities underlay a continuous circle of standing stones. When the tree was removed and burnt it is possible that a wooden post took its place, and charcoal was scattered around it. The pit was back-filled by the prehistoric builders and early reports suggest that a cist was inserted at the top, containing pottery, and possibly the small copper ring that we found. After this, the army used the mound as a firing point, and buried their spent blank cartridges there. The whole area was used for military manoeuvres during the Second World War; Italian prisoners re-surfaced the track leading from the village past the cairns to Blawearie house.

After the original establishment of the stone circle around the pit, and the in-filling of cobble stones, the place was so important that others were later buried in it by removing parts of the mound, constructing cists with some of the standing stones, and making good the disturbance by respecting the integrity of the circle. Thus the 'new' burials were incorporated with the old in unity.

The artefacts, carbon and soil samples and burnt bones were removed and analysed. The mound has been restored to what it might have looked like about 4,000 years ago, with the proviso that so many changes took place there that the reconstruction cannot represent all the episodes. There is a very detailed archive of the excavation at County Hall, Morpeth.

As you stand beside the mound of stones held in by the stone kerb, and look across to the Cheviot Hills and more immediate landscapes, no matter what the season, the site has an eloquent silence and stillness. The peace is shattered from time to time by low-flying aircraft, which use much of Northumberland for their training.

The excavation report and the archive are for future archaeologists to read and perhaps to reconsider. We are aware that our conclusions, based upon carefully recorded evidence, may be revised in the light of other discoveries or new techniques. What remains on the ground is an impressive monument that in about 30 years has blended into its surroundings; young heather and grasses grow around it and through the cairn stones. Sheep shelter and nibble grass there.

There are memories. During one autumn digging session we watched, as we worked, the clouds that had built up over Cheviot and shed their first snow, moving across the valley towards us. There was rain, and suddenly it ceased, leaving a rainbow that dipped into the centre of the cairn. An orange waterproof of one of the diggers vibrated with the spectrum. Long shadows raced across the valley and clouds dappled the scarpland. On another occasion an adder paid us a visit; many had not seen one before, and we all stood in a large circle around it to have a good look, then moved away to release it. The way to the site was a long trek up a hill from the minibus, after which we began the day with a briefing and the allocation of tasks. The excavation area had been marked and labelled, and we ensured that during the digging season everyone had a chance to excavate a different feature and to take part in recording. At the end of the day each group gave an account to the others on the results of its work. The caravan site office where structures and finds were recorded was also a shared workplace.

To cope with visitors we arranged for one person to take part of the day to greet them, to explain what was going on and to give them a photocopied leaflet. One lad developed a flair for this, offering to do more than his share; he must have been destined for the stage, and almost dragged passers-by to the site to explain with great enthusiasm what it was all about. At times his imagination ran riot, but no one seemed to mind.

We coped well with the press, radio and television. I remember a young reporter who arrived in light high-heeled shoes trying to cope with the steep hill, heather and eventually the difficulty of standing upright on a large spoil heap.

Long after the team had gone home for the night my co-directors and I discussed (or agonised over) the progress of the dig and the interpretation of what we were finding. After the bubbling excitement of so many young people at work, this was a time of great peace and reflection when the moorland closed in on us. In the first season we had to send the team home early because rain had made the work messy; as we stood on heather outside the 'cut' I felt through my soles that there was something hard beneath the heather, and we stripped off a square to reveal a small undisturbed cairn. This proved to cover a large cremation pit. In the same week a girl found what she thought was a hard sheep-dropping which turned out

The mid-point in the excavation of the cairns.

The young archaeologists move on, with a bumpy ride back to Old Bewick village, driven by the owner, John Wrangham.

to be the first of nine amber beads from a prehistoric necklace. A music student from London who came with the Conservation Volunteers was distressed because he thought he had broken the base off an inverted pot when it stuck to a flat stone that covered it. After reassurance that in this case the pot had been deliberately broken to admit cremations in antiquity, he was able to see what it covered: the pot full of cremated bone with a human vertebra visible at the top. The excavation of this pot became an event shared by the media, when friends who were professional archaeologists and the conservation officer joined us to remove it intact. After the compact 'natural' was cleared away, the pot stood proud, was wrapped in cling film held together by sellotape and then swathed with plastered cloth strips. It set like an iced cake, was detached from its pit base, and boxed in bubbled plastic for its journey to the British Museum where the rest of the Greenwell Collection is housed. The bones were returned to us for specialist examination.

Out of many other random memories, there is one that we turned into a video film of our High School team faced with the problem of moving heavy stones across loose earth. They learned that rollers were not the answer, for the stone kept sinking and would not move. We had casually left some planks lying around; the solution was to put the rollers on two planks arranged as tracks, lever the stone onto them and, with the help of fence posts, move it along.

One wonders what has become of all these young people, and what memories the excavation holds for them?

Cairns

Stamped with lichen, bound by bracken root,
Sunk in acid soil,
Each heap of stone affects disguise.
Death's ritual leaves slight signs.
Slanting sunlight, morning, evening,
Shadows each circumference. Betrays.
Many gouged by curiosity and greed.
First in rank and ostentation – first to fall;
The unpretentious huddle humbly in the soil, survive.
They are the scanty evidence of another life.
A smear upon the soil,
Burnt bone, a piece of flint, a pot, a bead,
Sealed once, but not invulnerable.
We focus on these tiny scraps of time
With force that hurls jet fighters overhead
And simulates the power of sun.
We are our Age, we bring technology
To bear upon a past where writing played no part,
But symbolism loomed large.

The completed site, now left to nature.

Gods lived and were placated;
Man and woman not enough.
Force drove through grass blades, crackled in the skies,
Hurled rainbows, hid the face of moon and sun.
Awesome. Kept us in our place.
We are the piece of broken bone, the pile of dust.
A piece of flint is our technology,
A bead or two our power or vanity.

We are the hands that placed the pot inside the grave,
Love that mourns a while.
The cairn above our heads cuts out the sky
As we move on.

HILL FORTS

The need for defence is a recurrent theme in history, and from the site of burial you may look towards the top of the scarp and see the serrated edge of the earthworks of a hill fort. Its profile is unusual, as it is the only 'double' hill fort in England. Others may show signs of modification, of increase or decrease in size, but here the expedient of building another enclosure against an existing one makes the fort look like a pair of half moon spectacles, the nose representing the junction of the two. Little is known about the forts, as the 'digging' has been fragmentary and inconclusive. There are some faint traces of circular huts and walling inside the enclosures, marked by a slight rise in the soil and a change in vegetation. There are two wartime pillboxes and a pond-like hollow in the base rock from which a millstone has been extracted. They are not the only enclosures in the area, for at the edge of the scarp, where a line of ageing trees forms a prominent landscape feature, is a smaller enclosure and two cairns, but nothing more can be said about them except that they are probably prehistoric too. Locals have referred to the hill fort for years as 'The Roman Camp' or 'The Ancient British Camp'.

The hill fort, like so many in Northumberland, is characteristic of the pre-Roman period, and may have served as a community centre, market, an animal enclosure, or religious site for the scattered farming and hunting communities, and not just for defence. Although there are many of these enclosures, little excavation has been done, and little is known of their origin, function and duration. We do know that they are the result of considerable effort: in this case soil had to be dug, stone had to be levered and shovelled out, the upcast piled between rows of stone to form ramparts, and the entrance gap plugged with a strong gateway. For what size of community was it built? What sort of effort went into it, and how many hours' work does it represent? Why are there two semicircles side by side? For how long was it in use? Perched on the edge of the scarp, it presents a formidable slope to an armed enemy attempting to climb up, and the strongest parts of the defences are concentrated where such natural advantages were weaker. Here the defences are in depth, with multiple ramparts and ditches ('multivallate'). It would not have proved a formidable obstacle to a Roman army, but may have been a fortress against clans of similar size to theirs. The Roman road runs below the scarp, and perhaps the fortress on the hill was abandoned or ignored. Perhaps each accepted the other's presence without having to fight locally?

There is another defensive enclosure on the moor, at *Corby Crags*, where the Harehope Burn cuts through the layers of sandstone to form steep cliffs. This is much simpler, with a small area enclosed by two ramparts and ditches, with an additional enclosure attached to it on the Blawearie side that may have been for animals. We do not know whether the two hill forts existed at the same time, or what the need for or relationship was between them. Corby Crags has in common with its larger neighbour a strong natural position, with the entrance at the most vulnerable side.

The Harehope Burn flows past on its way to join the River Aln, from a wide, gently shelving landscape that has over 40 cairns scattered over it. Where the burn is reached to the south the outcrops have formed a cave, known as *Cateran's Cave*, which means the cave of the outlaw, reiver, thief, and the area would have been useful to herd and hide stolen beasts.

Corby Crags 'hill fort'. This appears to have an extension for animals.

BLAWEARIE HOUSE

This part of the moor has one prominent ruined dwelling, Blawearie house, from which the cairns take their name. The house in its setting generates great power for all who visit it. One reason is the sheer size and shape of the outcrops around it, another is our response to things abandoned, and we wonder what made anyone want to live so far away from others. With its trees and cropped grass it contrasts from a distance with the heather and bent around it.

There may have been a prehistoric use of the site before it was cleared for building. It is such an outstanding natural feature in the landscape that it would at least have been a reference point for pastoral nomads and hunters. We know that the shepherds who lived here, the Rogerson family, made a collection of worked flint, jet and shale artefacts, some from the garden already established before them, and perhaps from some of the cairns on the moor. The house is built of easily quarried local freestone, but the garden walls and those built into the natural rock include cobbles, possibly taken from cairns. This is speculation.

The house is in three parts; a gabled two-storey building of the 'two-up-two-down' type, with two extra lower buildings attached. Whereas the main building has slate tiles, orange pantiles have been used for the hemmel. Little is known about the first owner, whose reasons for building so far away from other settlements can only be guessed. Others, including families with many children, lived there later, when it was necessary to be on the spot to be a good shepherd. Supplies had to be brought up the long trackway in the winter, which can be very bleak at this height.

The house has bricks in its structure, and some of these that are lying around have the stamp of *Straker and Love*. This firm flourished in Tyneside in the mid-nineteenth century. Bricks were often made as a by-product of mining; these came

Blawearie house: before the roof fell in. (*Birtley Aris*)

from the Howdon Colliery Company. As the company passed into the hands of River Tyne Commissioners in 1850, when Straker and Love left Howdon for the Durham coalfield, we have an approximate date for the building of the house. The Straker-Love partnership began in 1839. Mr Joseph Love was the junior partner, and began his mining life as a very young pit boy. A good businessman, he was also a good Methodist, and when he died in 1875 his personal estate was valued at nearly £1million. I heard from Stagshaw a curious rhyme about the two men, which I have not seen recorded:

> In Heaven above where all is Love
> You'll find no Strakers there.

What lies behind this is not known and it would not apply to the family generally! Whatever their fate and fortune, their names live on among the tumbled bricks of Blawearie. By another one of those coincidences, one of the Baker-Cresswell family that used to own land at Old Bewick, and gave me great help with my excavations in the county, including the Blawearie cairns, married into the Straker family near Warden. The house is set in a low-walled garden, with an outside 'netty' (short for 'necessity', a toilet). The water supply was from a spring many metres downhill, where water runs from rock to a trough that we re-excavated. The founder of the house turned the natural outcrops of sandstone into a garden, with walls, and made steps that led to little cleared areas. Trees and bushes remain from that period, but there were also flowers, vegetables and rhubarb.

In 1886 the Rev. E. J. Wilson in an article on Eglingham, the centre of the parish, wrote this:

At Blawearie is a sheep pen of considerable size whose walls are of solid rock some 15 feet high. On top of the huge wall is the large and well-cultivated garden of the obliging occupier. Natural arches, winding steps, tool house and garden seats are all cut out of solid rock.

In *The Fourth Friday Book* (1946) Paul Brown and his friend recorded a long walk up the hill to the house on a blazing hot day, and were met most hospitably by Mr and Mrs Faill, who lived there. They called this 'the promised land', made friends with the goats, hens, pigs and dogs, heard that the cow was a mile away because there was no grass nearer, and enjoyed tea. Their enthusiasm comes through the writing. They are not concerned with the house's history, but with the setting. There were gateposts leading into the great cleft in the rock, but no gate.

The whole place had at some time been converted into a big sheep pen, and a capital one, I imagine, it must have made. But that was not all. Steps had been cut at different places in the rock leading up to the gardens on the top. Rhododendron bushes and other cultivated things were still growing, although the gardens are not tended now as of yore. Here another plum tree was bearing a crop of fruit and there a fuschia which was in bloom. Who made the pen and gardens I cannot tell. It was really a remarkable and beautiful piece of work . . . I formed the idea that we were on the site of an ancient quarry. Did the stones for Old Bewick church come from it? There was once a tower at Bewick; where were the stones for building that quarried?

He ends his article by reflecting on life in 'out-by' places such as this, and how young people prefer to live in exciting towns when others are longing to 'go and live close to the earth.'

For people who had to work and live there without the amenities that lots of money can buy, this kind of romanticism may not cut much ice. We may love the ruin, and find the twisted bedding planes of the sandstone outcrops of great interest, but could we live there? One name that appears strongly in fragmentary records is the Rogerson family, who were shepherds here. Again, I find a connection; I have taught three of the descendants of this family. I remember the first time that I discovered the name carved into the massive stone in front of the house when I climbed it to get a better view. There is a wonderful picture given here of the family with a cobble stone wall behind them, by their house. Although the village school logbooks are not written as a social history, we can glean from them the pleasure and inconvenience of bringing children up in such a spot; the records are laced with references to snow storms, gales, rain, and we see that children in the area suffer from bronchitis, influenza, diphtheria, whooping cough, scarlet fever, and they get ringworm. Evacuees from Tyneside in the war years did not stay long. The children of Blawearie managed to get to school in all weathers, and were sometimes sent back because the tortoise stove in the school was again malfunctioning. More will be said about these logbook entries later.

Because the past has gone, and apparently cannot touch us again, we tend to view it kindly, and to look for good things, whereas it had the same mixture of good and bad as it is has for us. We can certainly enjoy Blawearie today, but we know little of the people who lived there—even some of their names. We can look from the ruins of the house through the mist towards the Harehope Burn, catch a glimpse of the slow flight of a heron, or the hovering and more frequent kestrel. Fewer larks each year rise in joy, and the wheatear (formerly the 'whitearse') flicks its tail up on the stones, even moving close to us for protection rather than face a sparrowhawk. One year we had to delay the excavation of part of the Blawearie cairn wall to allow a pied wagtail to hatch its young. Many robins have sung to us from the trees around the house. Bees home in on the thick heather in the autumn. For the recluse, seclusion would be from people amid abundant life on the moor.

The war years shattered the quiet. Spent mortar shells seem to have been cleared away now. The tracks of military vehicles mingle with those of the quarry carts and animals; from the air parts of the moor look like a railway junction. If a building is no longer useful, it dies. When I first saw Blawearie in the late 1960s the house still had its roof intact. No one lived there, no one cared for it, and it became dangerous to the hikers who still explored inside its walls. So the gable end was knocked down. Sheep shelter in the remains of the hemmels and happily nibble the grass that stands out so incongruously against the bent and heather. Much of the stone still lying around is of high quality, and from time to time someone disturbs an old rubbish dump, when an old kettle or broken plate surfaces for their inspection. We may regret that it has become a ruin, but it has ceased to be of use and is returning to the earth. It is abandoned, but dignified, and has taken on a new beauty. It joins many more such buildings in the Northumberland countryside. Where there are no commuters with cash to spend or people looking for second homes, where the composition of the farming community has changed and their numbers are very depleted, a remote building may die. Shepherds and herdsmen arrive on the moor in a variety of sturdy vehicles, but live elsewhere. Some farm workers never go on the moor.

This is not depressing. It is all part of the way time serves us, and we serve our time. In some ways it is good that no one has been allowed to build fences here and put up 'Private' notices. A generous landowner has allowed access well beyond the public footpaths, and for this reason we can enjoy everything that this place has to offer us. To get there, we have to make the effort of walking, we have to work for it, as the place is not handy for parking close by. We are all going to come away from it with something different, and I should be surprised if anyone came and felt nothing.

OLD BEWICK CHURCH

In Britain, many 'deserted' villages have resulted from changes in agriculture such as conversion from arable to pasture or to other changes in land use. Today the population of many rural areas has again shrunk; increased mechanisation is a major cause, for agriculture has ceased to be labour-intensive. As the countryside

Above and below: The Rogerson family in the grounds of their house.

has become depopulated small schools and shops have closed, and many other local services have suffered. Houses have been taken over as second homes or for retirement, or for tourism, which means that reliance on money and transport is paramount. Churches that once had large congregations find themselves struggling for survival, and many have been linked to a Team Ministry instead of having individual clergy. The Church has been a powerful focus in the life of rural communities, and for the Rites of Passage. It continues to be so for many.

To reach Old Bewick church, dedicated to The Holy Trinity, a narrow metalled lane leads along the Kirk Burn off the main road, the end of which has a cross. The church is half a mile from the village, and the site appears to have been chosen for its concealed position. It is a church of extraordinary beauty, but this is not immediately apparent from the outside. It looks rather like an oblong stone box with a bell tower that is puny. At the west end, closest to the gate, the quality of the building is seen in the massive stones built on the plinth that form the foundations, some with lewis holes in them. They appear to be older than its recorded Norman foundation. Were they recycled from an earlier building? The church was given by Queen Maud (or Matilda) to Tynemouth Priory around 1105.

At some stage the church suffered decline to such an extent that at the beginning of the nineteenth century it was unusable. The west wall shows the extent of the restoration in that century, for machine-cut stones are built up in courses on the older

Inside Old Bewick church.

ones, and two large lancet windows are incorporated. Above is a new tiled roof. To the north a vestry protrudes from the wall, and there is a distinct line where the walls have been raised to support the roof. The fabric includes an original Norman window and a broken piece of thirteenth-century grave slab.

It is the east end that has the earliest Norman feature of an apse with much of its original stone and later splayed buttresses joined to the apse by intriguingly-named 'squinched corbelling'. This apse is the sanctuary, and there are two restored small Norman windows set in it. As the apse curves round to the south side a third one of these small windows was removed in the fourteenth century and a larger squared one was inserted to admit more light, and to follow a fashion in which architects preferred to square off the east ends of the church. We see this at larger churches such as Holy Island Priory and Hexham Abbey.

A narrow door for the priest slits into the south wall, and the old stones that form the wall give way to a modern porch with louvered wooden doors that protects fragments of medieval stone. The graveyard is one of many found in Northumberland, but becoming rarer, where the headstones are still packed upright. The grave seen first as one comes through the gate proclaims *Vita Aeterna*—Life Everlasting. Other headstones are rich in the images of death and judgement, again so plentiful in county churchyards: the skull and crossbones, hourglass, scythe, and the open book. A more recent grave of 1918 announces on a metal plate that a young pilot cadet is 'SURE WINGED AT LAST AND FREE FULL FLEDGED ETERNALLY IN GOD'S ROYAL FLYING CORPS'. In the same area the master of a Masonic Lodge has all the attendant symbols on his metal memorial plate. Some recent headstones are massive, roughly hewn blocks of deeply buried stone brought down from the fell.

The churchyard is a grove with trees, bushes, hedges, flowers and birdsong. Under a yew hedge near the gate at the south-west end of the building is a curious grave stone with a very rudimentary angel with head and leaf-like detached wings. On the reverse, carved by someone not quite familiar with niceties of language and spacing, is the inscription:

> IN THE YEAR OF OUR LORD
> GOD 1770 HERE LIETH
> THE BODY OF ROGER WHO
> DEPARTED THIS LIFE
> AT BUECK MILL ROGER
> MUER 1770

The porch has a sundial marked 1742, re-erected on the gable and another on the ground with the date 1687. The doors open on a splendid medieval gravestone of a girl, with the main symbol of a pair of sheep shears. Opposite is a boy's triangular-sectioned grave slab with a sword and a cross. There are four parts of grave slabs, including another girl's grave and a re-used ornamented stone that became a holy water stoup.

The arch is older, Norman, with colonnettes, original block capitals and one section of rolled moulding of an arch. As the door opens, time stands still, as you must now. A sermon in stone? What words can describe simplicity? The walls that form the body of the church, whether old or new, blend into a powerful harmony of colour and texture, as though they have not been cut at all from the parent rock. An aisleless nave, tall, with high windows, leads to a rounded chancel arch, with Norman ornamentation, and rood screen slots. Two grotesque faces, open-mouthed with lots of teeth, separated by a rudimentary tree, grin from below the springing arch.

The apse arch, simpler, echoes the first in shape, and we are face to face with the dialogue of God and man at the altar. 'Holy, Holy, Holy, Lord God of Hosts' scrolls around the apse above a terracotta wall painted behind the altar. Above, the dome of the apse is painted blue with golden stars. It is surprisingly not incongruous.

We are impressed by the church's stillness, quietly withdrawn into itself, waiting. It has been saved, as a sketch in the church shows, from complete ruin. We see an act of gracious restoration in 1866-67 following an earlier one in 1695. There are details to linger over, such as a defaced effigy of a lady under a canopy, believed to have been made by an Alnwick sculptor in the fourteenth century. There is a frieze of saltire crosses that with other mouldings show that there was elaboration here when the church was first built.

The wall memorials tell us more about the Langlands family. John Charles was born on 27 March 1800, baptised in Newcastle on 16 October of the same year. The inscription in the church reads:

Became tenant at Old Bewick—May 1823. Fell asleep on the 11th day of March 1874. "Lord I have loved the habitation of thine house and the place wherein thine honour dwelleth."

His sons are commemorated and their memorials reflect the age:

The chancel and rose windows, are dedicated to the glory of God, and in memory of Mary, wife of John Charles Langlands, who died Aug: 30: 1852 aged 47 and of their son, Charles John Langlands, Ensign 43rd Light Infantry, killed in action, at the assault of the GatePah, Tauranga New Zealand April 29 1864 Aged 21.

In loving memory of John Shakespear Langlands, Major, 43rd Oxfordshire Light Infantry, Died 1895, at Longrood, Bilton, Warwickshire, in his 49th year. Also his son Alan Langlands, Lieut. 1st. Batt. South Wales Borderers, killed in action in France, May 9th 1915, in his 20th year.

His daughters are not commemorated in the church.

The scheme of restoration was initiated by Charles Langlands in 1862, and the church was reopened for worship five years later. Philip Hardwick, who designed part of the old Euston Station, wrote to him in 1851:

It fortunately happens in this case that so far from the destruction of any one portion of the church, a skilful restorer and one who took a real interest in the work would be able to replace every stone that had fallen and is still left on the ground . . . . The quality of the stone is excellent . . . The walls and arches that are still standing are in perfectly secure condition and the only part that need be positively taken down is the north west angle of the nave.

A suggestion he made was fortunately not taken up:

The Edward II window in the Apse so completely spoils the arrangement of the windows and is of so little interest in itself that it would be better removed and the original window restored, but it would be as well to leave the buttresses.

Mr Baker-Cresswell, the landowner, was approached in 1862 to help make the church something of use and not a memorial, and he, like others, contributed money to the project.

It is because so many loved this building and wanted it to lie again at the centre of the village, if not geographically, that it has survived ruin and the prospect of insensitive Victorian restoration. It is now one of the finest and most moving small churches in the county.

CHILLINGHAM

The neighbouring church of St Peter at *Chillingham* has much in common with Old Bewick, but the presence there of an outstanding 1443 tomb of Sir Ralph Grey and his wife Elizabeth links its fortune with that of the owners of Chillingham Castle and its estate.

The whole area is neat, well kept, and the castle a real attraction since the work carried out by its present owner, Sir Humphrey Wakefield. The parkland in which Chillingham is set was established in the thirteenth century, but the name refers to an earlier time (the settlement of Ceofel's people). The park is walled, and retains its ancient character.

Unlike other –*ingham* names in the county, Chillingham is pronounced with a hard *g* and the *ch* used to be pronounced *sh*. There is a saying locally that underlines the peculiarities of pronunciation:

The folk of Shatton say the sheese of Shatton is better than the sheese of Shillingham, but the sheese of Shatton's nee mair like the sheese of Shillingham than shalk's like sheese.

The castle, part of which is late thirteenth-century, was built in the fourteenth century on the plan of four towers connected by a wall, like Ford, for example. Within the park is a fortified cut down tower first mentioned in 1509. It is known as the Hepburn 'Bastle', and is roofless but otherwise in quite good condition. 'Hebron'

The Grey family monument in Chillingham church.

is the local pronunciation, and the spelling of the name from the thirteenth century onwards is *Hibburne* or *Hebburne*. This tower now brings us back to Old Bewick.

OLD BEWICK TOWER

Small fortifications were dotted liberally all over Northumberland, speaking of turbulence, insecurity, and the need for defence, even of very small settlements. They were not intended, as castles were, to resist armies and siege tactics, but were important places of refuge where smaller raids could be resisted or where small bands of armed men could congregate before a raid. Many have survived, some as parts of buildings that have incorporated them in their more peaceful domestic structures, when the pressure of war eased off. We know the names of many of these strongholds, and Old Bewick had one, now buried beneath the road.

First mentioned in 1514, it could hold a garrison of 40 men. As the township belonged to the Prior of Tynemouth before the dissolution of the monasteries, it reverted to the ownership of the Crown. In 1539 the bailiff was Gilbert Collingwood, who did not render any accounts 'because it was kept entirely for the defence of the Lordship in time of war'.

From scraps of evidence, we know that the roof of the tower had been made of lead and by 1541 any building outside it was in disrepair. By 1584 it was a ruin, but must have still been used because the bailiff was accused in 1614 of imprisoning people in it to extort money from them. In 1584 the Commissioners had reported that it was the Queen's property, and that a barmkin should be built 30 yards square enclosed by a stone wall, and that stabling for fifty horses should be added. The accession of James VI of Scotland to the English throne as James I began to ease the tension of the borderlands, but in 1608 a survey describes it as:

> a faire stronge tower, with a garth (yard) and a dovecote of hewen stone, which has been wholly covered with leade but most part of the lead is now decayed or purloyned away whereby it is not habitable but in one corner that is vaulted over. This tower hath commonly been a refuge for the Tenants in time of danger.

Towers like this were either remodelled or became quarries. This one lingered rather sadly, and became the home of Alice Ramsey. In 1676 her husband was dead, and she complained that her son who inherited the tower treated her badly:

> She lived in the tower of Old Bewick for one year ending on Whitsunday last. The leads and timber were so ruinous that the rain came in and she could not live in the said tower. Since her removal John Ramsey caused take lead of the tower.

Two years later it was referred to as 'the manor house'; it was described as not being habitable for some time, and 'only two or three poor people lived in some of the rooms thereof, and some of them paid 4s a year for the rooms they lived in.'

Apparently in 1866 some old people could still remember the ruins after the road had been built over it at the south end of the village. Jim Clark told me that when a wall was demolished in a field to the west of the site there was among the masonry some fine, well-cut and shaped stone that could have come from this building, and that existing walls still bear traces of it.

HISTORY THROUGH LOGBOOKS

Although 'reading' the landscape and buildings can give us a good picture of the past, documents are essential to our knowledge. Even so, we can only know in part about the past. Old Bewick school has become part of the recycling process of history; it is now a residence at the north end of the village. A date of 1870 and the Baker-Cresswell logo of a squirrel give a firm reference point for its foundation. What happened there is still alive in some people's memories and in logbooks. Not often used, such sources may give us an insight into life; the Old Bewick logbooks cover about a century. In them, school headteachers were expected to record day to day events, such as attendances (by which schools were judged), visitors, reports of inspections, incidence of disease, and to make comments on curriculum. The type of entry depends on the personality and outlook of the writer. The school, like so many other small rural schools, was closed in June 1960.

What sort of picture are we given of this rural area? Extremes of weather, especially snowfalls, heavy rain and wind were a preoccupation of the teachers; attendance was affected, and the conditions of work in the classroom, as the stove might not cope. Children were afflicted with diseases. The harvest and the shooting season also kept children off school. The hiring system meant a new batch of children coming to be educated, some of whom were well behind in their education. What follows gives brief glimpses of these things.

In the 1860s we find that Mr Langland's daughters took an active part in the school, teaching needlework, singing, and reading from the bible. Notation, dictation, reading and geography accounted for much of the rest of the curriculum.

On 19 April there were 35 pupils. Among the adults, Sybilla, Margaret, Fanny and May Langlands were busy with the artistic subjects and reading, but the system came in for criticism; subtraction and notation were bad: 'Standard 1 form the small letters very badly'. Dictation was also bad. The headteacher came to this conclusion in a period of self-doubt that came before the harvest. Holidays were from 12 August to 12 September and the headteacher knew that schoolwork would be forgotten. By December, though, the school inspector was happier, although he wrote that 'I saw this school under great disadvantage, as it was very much thinned by illness, and the roads were almost impassable with snow.' There were only 16 children there.

Standards were affected by the weather and by the mobility of population. Teachers

Old Bewick school in 1897, in commemoration of Queen Victoria's Diamond Jubilee.

could work hard on one group, which would then 'flit.' Others would come in. Three boys of 6, 7, and 9 came 'and not one of them knew the alphabet.' Yet a 5-year old girl came in June 1872 who knew all the alphabet, but by the next month 'Nearly all the children who have entered since May can now spell out little words.'

The Inspectors were aware of these difficulties, which must have been common in all parts of the county. In 1871 when the children were beginning to use paper as well as slates, he reported, 'The school has suffered from the changes of farm labourers during the year. Notwithstanding these, the results of the examinations are fairly creditable.'

Occasionally the teacher broke into despair:

> It is utterly impossible to make my regular advancement in classwork . . . The average of the week is 35, the largest we have had for a long time. The work is a long way back, each of the children having done nothing since before harvest.

Two months after this entry he writes: 'Miss Langlands gave the children their annual treat of teacake today. Mr Langlands presented a prize to every child who had twenty Sundays at school during the year.' Perhaps this is why the Diocesan Inspector of this church school found the scripture so satisfactory throughout as well as the repetition of hymns and selected chapters of the catechism.

The staff of the school changes; by 1882 the beautiful copperplate of one head is replaced by a more flamboyant style, each entry underlined with a most incredible series of squiggles. The vocabulary changes too, with a distinct liking for words like 'zealous' and 'diligent'. There were 21 boys and 15 girls. When the Inspector called in January 1882, he was baffled somewhat because one or two bright scholars in standard 1 'would answer the questions first, and the remainder joined in collectively after the lead had been so given'. Standard 2 made no attempt to answer, but in standard 3 the New Testament work had been thoroughly prepared and was the best work presented in that grade.

March brought sickness and cold and stormy weather. It also brought a far from complimentary report from the HMI who wrote, amongst other things: 'The reading was very fairly correct (very fairly?) but there was no modulation. The Dictation was below par throughout. The Composition was weak. The Handwriting was very fair' . . . and so on. Fair, with modifications, was his in-word.

May, June and July were months when the weather should have removed one excuse for non-attendance at school, but the log entries show that this was not the case. The number of farm sales, flitting, a supposed outbreak of scarlet fever which turned out to be a false alarm (and even then the children didn't return) account for some absences, but on July 14 the head wrote, 'The bad attendance is now having a serious effect on the work of the school.' Some of them were helping with the hay harvest, and just as things were beginning to improve and attendances rise, down came the rain, out came chills and bronchitis, and down went attendance. In August 'Owing to the children absenting themselves during hay leading, and going about idling' all was not well.

Ten years on, in 1892, school began with everyone present except a boy with a scalded foot. The Archdeacon, a realist, consented to close the school for two days at the end of the week 'as half the children would be absent owing to the shooting'.

There were severe snowstorms, but a slight lull allowed R. Matthews to come from Harehope Hall to give the children tea and cake. 'I had the room tastefully decorated for the occasion. Miss Berkley presided at tea and gave the children two toys each. The curate was present, and after tea, games were indulged in till 6.30 p.m.' It was no doubt a pleasant interlude, but colds kept children away from school. The stove wasn't hot enough to keep the school warm, even though it burned all night. It was repaired.

There was whooping cough, and in February when examinations were held there were only 17 children present. The Inspector felt that the head hadn't been long enough at the school to make his mark, and had received no account of what had been done before he came. Shortly after these comments, a boy fell and knocked his kneecap off, but was soon back at school after a visit to the bonesetter. Not for long though, as violent snowstorms closed the school.

The teacher looked after the school too. He cut a drain and cut ventilators in the door of the office. The snow continued in March.

When the school ended for the year, we are provided with a list of songs for 1892:

1. The Harp that once through Tara's Hall
2. On brave boys!
3. The Coral Insect
4. Gently gliding o'er the stream and
5. The Soldier's Motherless Daughter.

It was decreed that 'The singing will be taught by the Tonic Solfa method for the first time.'

Recitations for 1893 were:
Standards 1 and 2 'Casabianca'; Standard 3. 'Inchcape Rock'; the rest, 'Lochiel's Warning'.

So there we have a glimpse of some items of the equivalent of the National Curriculum of the day.

The children came from a defined catchment area, with a population of about 150. The places were Old and New Bewick, Nursery Hill, Bewick Bridge, Bewick Folly, Blawearie, Quarry House and Hangwell Law. As an example, we have seen the house at Blawearie (also spelt *Bloweary* and *Blaw Weary*), and we now know that in that limited accommodation as many as ten people lived there.

In 1902 there were 127 people in the area, of whom 38 were on the school register, There were 12 under 5s, 2 under 4s, 2 under 3s, 5 under 2s, and 3 babies. It is impossible to examine all the entries here, but a selection will be of interest and keep the story moving:

March 1907.	There was a marked improvement in the children's work. Geography is approached more liberally and in an 'intelligent manner'. The library is receiving attention.
January 1908.	'Some of the children at Blaweary have whooping cough, so I sent the scholars from there home this morning.'
May 1909.	'9 scholars withdrawn owing to their parents leaving the district.'
January 1910.	'The snow has fallen heavily all day and is drifting. Five of the children present are from a distance, 2 from Blaweary and 3 from Harehope Lodge, and as there is no sign of the storm abating, I think it is advisable to send them home at 2.30.'
July 1910.	An HMI report finds the teaching sympathetic, much of the work satisfactory and on common sense lines, but 'in certain directions considerable improvement can be looked for.'
May 1918.	'Instead of the first lesson on the timetable for this afternoon, I took the scholars to examine the Ancient British camp on the hill.' There is no reference to the Great War.
April 1920.	An HMI report shows that there is now a woman at the helm. 'This is a very pleasant little school. The excellent influence of the Mistress is apparent in the good behaviour of the children and in their attitude towards their work.'
April 1923.	Two pupil teachers began work in September.
July, 1928.	'Instead of the first lesson on the timetable this afternoon, the upper division was taken to examine the church. Children made notes and sketches after the teacher pointed out interesting features in the building.'

The HMI is surprised that 'many of the children seem to have a poor knowledge of the animal life of the district. He notes a falling off in spoken English. 'The enunciation of many of the elder children is so slovenly that they are almost inaudible, and several of them are unable to reproduce in even two or three connected sentences the subject matter of chapters in books they have recently read.' He also says: 'It is a pity that in a school where both the teachers are women there should be no woman Manager'.

The number of children on the roll rose from 31 in 1929 to 36 in 1930. There were 25 in 1932 and 30 in 1933. In these years the inspectorate was still going on about the inability of the children to speak clearly.

Perhaps it is better not to dig more deeply into the records, as they concern people whom they may affect today, so to bring this account back to the beginning of the section we have this:

September 3, 1937. Standards IV-VII visited the Roman Camp on Bewick Hill this afternoon, made sketches and collected wild flowers on the way back.

PEOPLE AND PLACES TODAY

Today the landscape has changed, particularly by the forestry planting on the western slopes of Hepburn Moor, from the scarp downwards. There is a notice that reads 'Hepburn Wood Walks' and I am tempted to ask 'And does Burnham Wood come to Dunsinane?' Some of the moorland has been converted to pasture. Forestry here is associated with the work of Frederick ('Fritz') Berthele, who was a German prisoner during the last war, and chose to stay. He married Joan, a local girl who was at one time a pupil at Old Bewick school. Their daughters went to school with mine, at the Duchess' Girls' High School in Alnwick. It was through the friendship of our daughters that I first met Joan and Fritz at their cottage at Hepburn. I was soon to discover that he had an interest in prehistory manifested in one of the finest collections of flint implements that anyone has ever amassed in the north, ranging from the Mesolithic to early Bronze Age. It includes some pottery fragments and beads of rare quality. This was the result of searching newly-ploughed moorland throughout the county prior to planting, land unlikely to be touched again for many years; the collection can be seen in Chillingham Castle. I was taken to many sites on the moorlands where burial cairns lay, and in one of the deep furrows made for forestry there was a triangular piece of sandstone covered with cup marks. Many people have stopped at their cottage, have been made welcome, and were able to see and handle the artefacts. I was able to borrow some of them for use in schools and evening classes. Fritz's services to forestry, his work in the Trade Unions, and the strength of his presence earned him the British Empire Medal from the Duke of Northumberland on behalf of the Queen. As for archaeology, the devotion required to collect so many implements came home to me when, after a whole day out together, we found only one flint flake!

Fritz was a member of the Chatton Leek Club when he invited me to speak there many years ago. Everyone in the village seemed to be there, including babes in arms. After the slides and chat that I gave them, a local shepherd, Jim Robson, offered me photographs of panels of rock art that I did not know about. He had found them on Amersidelaw Moor, next to Chillingham whilst shepherding on horseback, where I went with Fritz (and later a TV team) to record them. Since then he has found others. History becomes very personal in Northumberland. The farming community is greatly interested in its own area, and sharing it is a two-way process based on trust.

When we excavated the Blawearie Cairns, the late Edward Wrangham and his manager, Jim Clark, not only provided tractors to transport all our equipment up the hill for four years, but they also provided stakes, rollers and wedges so that our young people could experiment with moving large stones around.

This trust and co-operation between archaeologists and people who own or work on the land is one of the outstanding features in Northumberland; at least, I have found it so.

2

Name this Place

Each name of village, town and farm has a locked-in history that would not otherwise appear in the record. Some give up meanings fairly easily; Northumberland was land north of the Humber. Others have pronunciations that that do not at first seem to have much to do with spelling; Ulgham (pronounced Uffm) originated as *ule-hwhamm* and means an owl corner or nook. Ashington in 1170 was *Essende*, *aescen-denu*, a valley overgrown with ash trees long before its expansion into a large mining area and housing estate. Cramlington, *Cramlingtuna* in 1130, may mean a spring associated with cranes, now a New Town. These names all have Old English roots. The Romans, despite their garrisons here, left very little in the language, and Latin comes to us through Norman French, also largely absent from our place names.

From maps we are able to picture settlements located at special places: at a stream bend, deep valley, round hill, cliff, flat alluvial land by a river, or a thick forest. Badgers, deer, foxes and wild cats are in such numbers that places are named after them. The names of family groups of settlers may be their only historical record, with indication of the vegetation they encountered and then crops that they grew. Swamps, reeds, brightly-glittering streams, bare hills, wooded slopes, heavy clay land, pastures, beanfields, thorn bushes, farms where there were bees or geese, fields of barley, sheepfolds, pastures, or places where heather grows create a colourful canvas in their word picture. Ancient burial cairns, fortified camps and roads are named.

To interpret accurately what a place name means is a study that involves documentary research and knowledge of languages. Many have common suffixes such as *ham*, *ton* and *wick*, all with the general meaning of a place where people settled. These parts of names are called 'elements', of which there can be one or more. People coming to Northumberland for the first time may have some difficulty with a list like this: Edlingham, Eglingham, Ellingham. Local pronunciation of 'ingham' is *injum*. The same applies to Bellingham. The differences in the first element in the words are that each refers to a different group of families.

Edlingham	Eadwulfincham (1050)	Eadwulf's people's homestead.
Eglingham	Ecwulfincham (1050)	Ecgwulf's people's homestead.
Ellingham	Ellingeham (1130)	Ella's people's settlement.

Personal names appear in many place name elements, such as: Warkworth (Werce), Bamburgh (Bebba), Adderstone (Eadred), Rothbury (Hrotha), Throckrington (Thoker), Titlington (Titel), Simonside (Sigemund) and Bavington (Babba).

Rothbury and Bamburgh both have the element *burgh*, *burh*, which means a fortified place. Brough Law has the same element: a fortification on a hill. Dunstanburgh combines a hill (*dun*) with *stan* (stone) and *burgh* (fortification), descriptive of an impressively situated castle, perhaps with an earlier site beneath it, on the top of a whinstone outcrop. Other fortified places take the element *chester*, applied to pre-Roman and Roman fortifications, from the Latin *castra*, through Old English *ceaster*, *caester*. Rochester (*Roff* in 1208) is Hrofi's Roman fort, or it could be from *hroc*, a rook's fort. If the latter, it could symbolise its abandonment, just as Craster (*Craucestre*, 1242) is an old fort inhabited by crows.

Crow or ravens appear in other place names, such as Cawledge and College Burn (crow's ledge), Corby's Crags and Crawley (Crow's Hill).

A *Law* can mean either a hill or a burial cairn. *Heugh* is a cliff as in Ravensheugh. *Dun* is also a hill (as in Warden), but sometimes its spelling changes because it is like *den*, which is a valley, often alongside a hill. Dunstan is a hill of stone. Blagdon (*Blackedenn*) is black valley; Deanham (*Danum*) is settlement in a valley.

Hills produce some interesting names; Humbleton in the Cheviots is bareheaded (*hamel*); Skirl Naked may mean that the hilltop is bright or shining.

On the hill slopes springs (*kelda*) may gush out. Akeld is the oak-covered place at the spring (*Achelda*). It is not, as one popular story has it, the place where someone fleeing from the aftermath of the Battle of Flodden declared that they were all killed. Legends develop in an attempt to account for something difficult to explain, such as sites attributed to the Devil or to Caesar, but they are also made up to explain a place name. Although Weldon Bridge on the River Coquet means a spring valley (*wielle denu*), there is a story of a band of marauding Scots looking for Brinkburn Priory to sack it, which a thick mist prevented them from doing. The monks were so thankful for their deliverance that they rang the bell in joy. The Scots were thus guided to them, sacked the priory and returned to their leader at a place where he said 'Well done'.

Blanchland is another religious foundation, but whereas the name Brinkburn is Old English, Blanchland is French (1165 meaning white glade). 'Priest' enters names such as Preston Tower (*preosta-tun*, the priest's land), and Priestpopple is a Hexham street where 'popple' (also *pightle*, *paffle*, and *poffle*) is a small enclosure.

Natural vegetation and farming give their names too. Allerwash had alders. Birch trees appear in places like Birkenside (1262), and beeches at Bockenfield and Bitchfield. There were elders at Ellenford, lime trees at Linsheeles. Bolam owes its name to tree trunks (*bolum*). Eshott (*Esseta* in 1186) is an ash grove. Espley was an aspen wood. Broomley, Broomhaugh were covered with broom. Clennell was a 'clean' hill, free of weeds. At Swarland (1242) the land was *swaer*, difficult to plough. Thorneyhaugh was covered with thorns, Fairnley a ferny grove. Ingram (1242 *Angerham*) and Angerton (1186) were covered with grass. Beans grew at Beanley, clover at Clavering and Clarewood (*claefre*). Fenton and Fenwick were marshy, and Morwick was a farm on the edge of wasteland. At one stage Felton (*Feltona*, 1167) was a farm in open country, an area larger than a *leah* or ley.

Grindon was a green, a grassy spot. At Haining the land was enclosed for meadow. At Aydon there was hay, rosehips at Hepple, holly at Hulne Park Alnwick, Linacres grew flax, there was good pasture for cows at Melkridge, rye at Ryal (rye hill). Roddam and Riding Mill were clearings. Elishaw had a thicket. *Strod* in Broadstrothers Burn meant that the land was overgrown with brushwood, whereas at Weetwood the land was wet.

Although Haltwhistle has a railway station this has nothing to do with its meaning. *Hautwisel* in 1240 comes from Old English *heafod*, a hill, and *twisla/twisel* is the fork in a river; here the high ground overlooks a place where two streams join. The English army crossed Twizell Bridge on their way to Flodden in 1513. Capheaton (*Magna Heton* in 1242) is from *hea-tun*, a settlement on high ground. Cambo (*Camho*, 1230) is the spur of a hill with a crest; Cambois, pronounced 'kamus', was *Cammes* in 1050, and is a crooked, curving bay. Holborn is a stream in a hollow, sunken place; Wooler has nothing to do with sheep, but is a stream bank (*Wullore*, 1187). Shaftoe is a shaft-shaped ridge. There was a mere or lake at Boulmer (Bulemer 1161), so the place probably means a bullock's or bull's shallow rock pool on this coast.

Animals and birds appear in the names. Hartburn (stag), Harehop, Swinhoe (wild boar), Shipley (sheep), Tod Hill (fox), Brockbushes (badger), are self-evident. There are cows at Kyloe, deer at Heatherslaw (*Hedaereslawa* 1176, *Headeor*—stag or deer hill).

Scrainwood (*Scravenwood*, 1242) is the Old English *sreawena wudu*, the wood of the shrewmice or villains. Wooden had wolves, Raylees roe deer, Callaly calves.

Among the birds are cocks on the River Coquet, woodcocks at Rugley, eagles at Yarnspath Law, a cuckoo at Gowk Hill, and hawks at Gled Law and Hawkshill.

One of the most important ancient sites is Yeavering. It was Adgefrin, Adgebrin in 730, from the Welsh *gafre*, a goat. Wild goats are still to be seen there. The name Gateshead has the same origin.

FIELDS

Every field in the county has, or has had, a name. These names, unlike those of those of towns and villages, frequently change; new owners may rename the fields, boundaries change, and maps are lost. The attractive and informative hand-painted maps by Robert Norton in the period 1580–1630 for the Earl of Northumberland are a particularly valuable source of names, especially as the Earl's continued ownership of the land enables us to trace some subsequent changes.

Names given to fields are a great source of detailed, personal history of the land. Fields come in all shapes and sizes, mostly enclosed with fences, hedges and walls. This has not always been so; some of our earliest field systems are terraces (lynchets) still to be seen in the Cheviot Hills and at places like Warden and Corbridge. It is now thought that terraces pre-date the Roman occupation and continued in use through the medieval period. Also in pre-Roman times was a system known as 'cord-rig', narrow strips of ploughland close together.

The usual earlier pattern is a more open system than we see today, with large areas around the vill or township divided into strips that were shared among the community, giving a share of fertile and less fertile land. Farming these scattered strips demanded co-operation, and mobility. A three-course rotation system maintained the fertility of the land, allowing some to recover and to be manured. Outside was the common land where people were given the right to graze fixed numbers of animals (in 'stints'). Having scattered strips gave way gradually to a more efficient system of grouping strips of land together in one holding; plague and war would often accelerate this when there were fewer people to farm the land. By 1800 most of Northumberland was 'enclosed' and the fields looked much as they do today. The Earl's surveys show the pattern of the open-field system, which is retained in many cases. The big open fields are defined and named, and within them the strips of land are drawn. When the strips, later defined by 'rig and furrow' ploughing, were turned over to grass, there is a fossilised arable system that we see in many parts of the county, especially in low light or under a light covering of snow. There is later rig and furrow, some narrower than the medieval type, and others made with modern machinery in straight lines. The old system, with its S-profile curves, was the result of using ploughs attached to oxen, which needed a wide turn at the headlands. Soil built up on the rig, and the furrow grew deeper, which assisted drainage and corrugated the land to give a slightly higher temperature than a flat surface. The open-field system has a vocabulary that partially survives. A field was divided into a group of furlongs, separated by a headland, or balk. One furlong, the length of a furrow, was made up of bundles of strips variously named as acre, land, rigg, selion and dale. A furlong is also called a flatt, furshott or sheth.

It is the personal history behind the naming of fields that is fascinating and tantalising. Labour in Vain, Little Sloshes, Canada, Botany Bay, Klondyke, Grimping Haugh, Cork Leach Ley, Hot Bog, Niddles, Armourer's Fall, The Boiling Riggs, Bodle Hole Quarter, Blakehopesburnhaugh, Crum Roods, Fislebee Pasture, Corney Horners, Hungerful Lases, Haughslopp Butts, Moralees, Seggy Hole and East Toddles have their own poetry. These I have selected from hundreds that I recorded for my published work in 1977.

A study of field names is within everyone's grasp. The beginning is a large-scale map, amicable contact with a farmer/landowner, and a walk over the land. Present names can be pencilled in; the next step is to check with county records and other sources to see if there are earlier maps of the same area. Many maps have been lost; others have numbered fields but no keys to the names. Sometimes a valuable new source may be found. This happened to me when I lived in Felton; in the 1770s Thomas Bell produced detailed estate maps, and in 1976 the owners of Felton Park gave me his maps of the Riddell estates. They were drawn in ink on paper, and then stuck down on linen in a book. It had been passed around the village and had suffered in the process, but I was able to give it to the Records Office, where it remains. Local contacts are essential; when I researched the Eshott fields, the owners were able to provide me with information from maps of 1877 and 1976. The changes in names give a salutary lesson when one tries to understand what they mean. High Seas replaced The Tofts because a lady was moved by the sight of the wind rippling a field of grain. March Brown was thus named after a friend of the family who marched rather than walked everywhere. Quality Walk replaced Great West Field because this was where the people of 'quality' chose to walk.

These examples help to show that one may be wrong about the origin and meaning of a name. Ewart Park, near Wooler, is an area rich in archaeology, and when a friend found a field name Spears, I had to point to the possibility of its coming from Old English spearcas, meaning that it was covered with brushwood.

Sources such as the Alnwick maps of 1580–1630, contained in massive volumes, are not only outstanding for the maps alone, but for the beautifully written lists of every acre, rood and perch of land and who owned or farmed it. There we have an enormously important archive. Field name study brings us close to the land, its vegetation, birds and animals, and farming practices, and names people who would normally not be in written history.

Of all the interesting maps available, I have chosen one of Acklington, where there is now a prison on the site of an RAF base, adjoining opencast coal mining, yet still retaining a village plan recorded by Robert Norton as part of the area that extends through Warkworth and Buston to the former grain port of Alnmouth. The map is a redrawn Tithe map of the mid-nineteenth century.

There follow examples taken from the map to illustrate what kind of information is given:

Physical features: Bank Head Field, Sandy Burn Field, The North Haugh (alluvial land by water), Moor Crooks (bends), Fairney Hill Banks (ferns), Thistley Moor, Whinny Moor (gorse), Soddy Brig Close (marshy enclosure at the bridge), The Rush, The Long Brocks (brooks), Hoeings, Small Holdings, and The White Moor (not a reference to soil colour but to white grass).

Position: Felton Field (near another village), North Moor, West and East Cleveley Close, Cheeveley North Moor, South Lands, West and East North Field, Far and Near Acklington Stile, North and South Low field, Middle Front Field, Before the Doors, Back of the House.

Agriculture: Little Hay Fields, The Barley Field, East Havels and West Ravels (both referring to havers, oats – thus haversack), Hills of Grain, Meadow Field, the Orchard

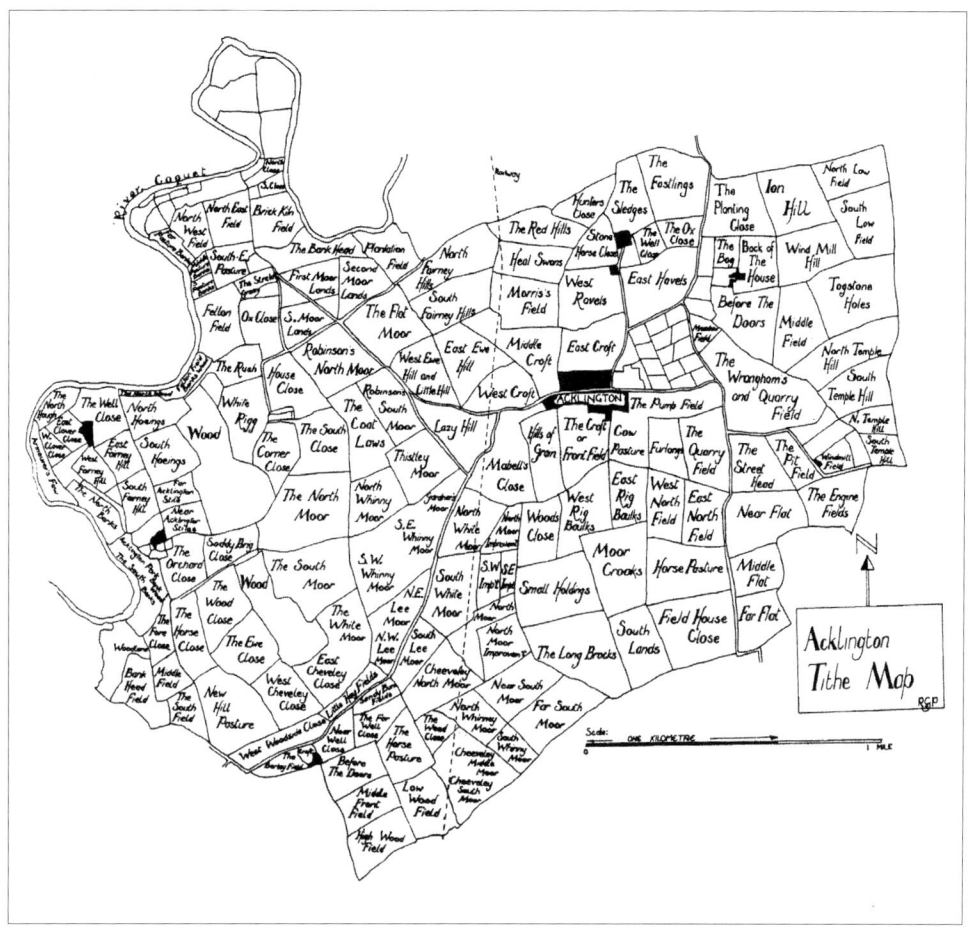

Acklington Tithe map. (*Re-drawn by Richard Parkin*)

Close, The Ewe Close, Plantation Field, Lazy Hill, The Ox Close, East and West Rig Baulks (referring to the rig and furrow system of ploughing), Furlongs, The Horse Pasture and North and South Improvement.

Industries: Brick Kiln Field, Windmill Hill Field, The Quarry Fields, The Engine Fields, The Whimseys (winding engines drawn by horses), The Pump Field, The Pit Field, Togstone Holes.

Personal names: Hunter's Close, Robinson's North Moor, Gardner's Moor' Morris's Field, Ion Hill, Mabell's Close, The Armourer's Fall and Heal Swans.

Others: The Street Head, South and North Temple hill, The Rey hills, The Fastlings, The Sledges.

THE LOWER COQUET VALLEY

To illustrate place names, a section along the Coquet valley is drawn from Rothbury to the port of Amble.

Rothbury lies at the heart of Fell sandstone country, a very attractive village with an Anglian foundation that is reflected in the extraordinary cross now used partly as the base of the font in the church, the rest being in the Museum of Antiquities in Newcastle. The village architecture is mostly nineteenth and twentieth century, reflecting its popularity among visitors. Lord Armstrong chose the area to build his house at Cragside. There is no Domesday survey of Northumberland, so place names have to be found in other early sources. Rothbury is *Routhebiria* in 1125, and means either Hrotha's fortification or the red one. The most obvious fortifications visible are a string of fortified enclosures of the Iron Age overlooking the River Coquet on the north and south. At Lordenshaw in particular one of these is accessible, with the added bonus of some fine prehistoric rock art on National Park land. The river was *Cocwud(a)* in 1050 and *Coqued* in 1104–08, meaning Cock's Wood, presumably after the abundance of wild fowl.

The river cuts deeply through carboniferous sandstones, shales, limestones and coals that are exposed in many places, and were the basis of a number of small local industries, including a short-lived iron smelter at Brinkburn. The valley has spectacular scenery, and the Augustinians chose a lovely sheltered spot for their Priory on the brink of the river. In the sandstone cliffs that you see on the way down, tree roots have forced their way through cracks to form some extraordinary shapes. The river first passes by Pauperhaugh, usually pronounced 'Popperhoff' or 'Papperhoff'; it was *Papwirt halgh* in 1120, meaning Papworth's Haugh. Where the river bends or has flat land on either side, the alluvial stretches so formed have the local term 'Haugh' to describe them. As the river flows east and northeast this phenomenon appears in a number of names. As the river nears Felton, Shothaugh and Elyhaugh appear in the narrow, steep valley, the steepness announced by Catheugh, a wild cat cliff, Middleheugh and Brinkheugh. In Shothaugh, although we have no early spelling of this, 'shot' comes from O.E. *sceat*, a block of land with its selions running in the same direction, and a turning place or headland for the ploughteam. Elyhaugh has the element O.E. *ea*, a river, or M.E. *ele*, and island. Names such as Ponteland have the same element. Beyond Felton, where the land widens and where there would have been large open fields, Mouldshaugh, although it has no early documentation, could contain 'moldi' or 'mold', a small hill, which it stands on before the land slopes down to the river. Brainshaugh, *Bresegne* in 1104, is either from *borrans*, a burial mound, or it is Bregwine's haugh.

To the west of Felton the river is fed by the Millstone Burn, named for obvious reasons, and the Swarland Burn. Swarland is given a name that shows that the land was heavy to plough.

Between the tributaries and the main river is Longframlington, stretched along the village road that takes its name from an early settler, Framela and his people (*Fremelintun* in 1166). Other villages that lie to the north of the Coquet have a

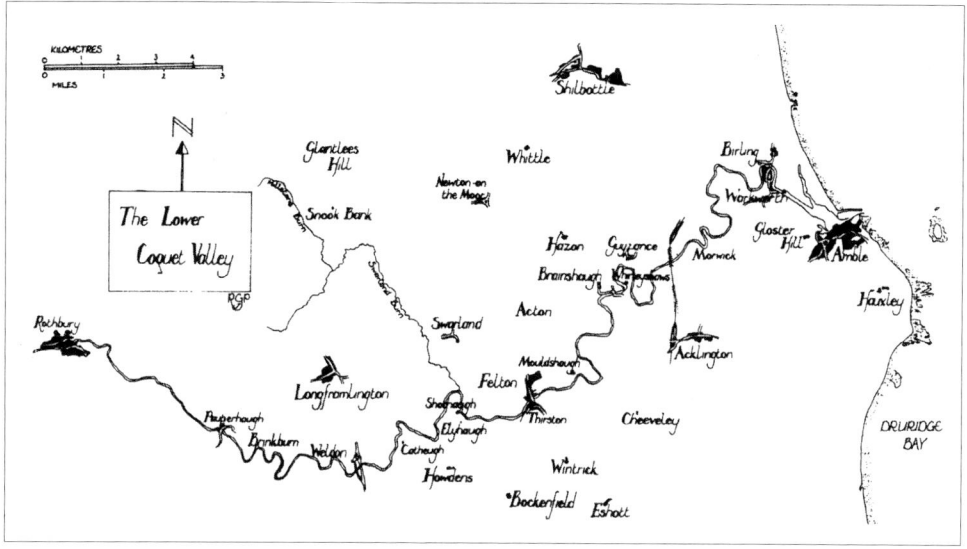

Map of the lower Coquet Valley. (*Richard Parkin*)

Brinkburn Priory.

variety of origins. The abandoned coalfield area centred on the medieval village of Shilbottle is from Scipleaingas-botl, the Shipley people's building.

Whittle was a hill covered with whitened grass, Acton with oak trees; Hazon (Heisende in 1170) was probably the hedge's end, a boundary.

Two names of special interest are Guyzance and Whirleyshaws; the former is a rare name *Gynis*, named after Guines, near Calais, and the latter, although it well describes the swirling course of the river at the place, actually comes from Quirlecharr, possibly with the less romantic meaning of a quarry.

Felton is a major crossing place of the Coquet, and until the recent by-pass was built, it took the A1 traffic through its main street, once packed with inns, having its own brewery and gas works, over its attractive fifteenth-century bridge up a steep hill to Thirston. Here the name was *Thrasfriston* in 1242, meaning the place was settled by Thraesfrith and his people. Around are names such as Bockenfield and Eshott, where beech trees and ash trees grew, where farming mixes with microlight flying, and where Felton village has developed good quality housing in the commuter belt. Within its bounds is Gasworks Farm, and old water mill that was made to work when I lived in the village, and a church that is still an architectural puzzle. The bank and reading room and chapel closed long ago, but a rich variety of architectural styles remains.

Sign posts challenge us to seek meanings of places.

Felton village from the west. Felton Park is in the foreground.

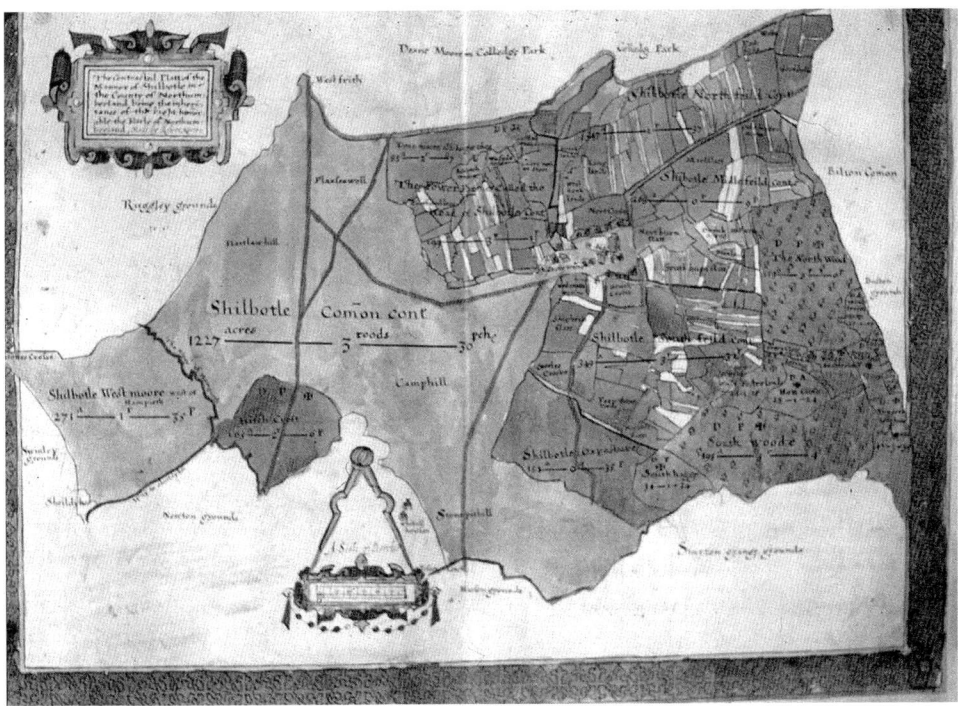

Shilbottle township in 1620

Warkworth Castle

The river bends frequently on its course to the coast. At Morwick (*Morewic* in 1161), a farm on the fen, the sandstone cliffs near to the fording place of the river and the site of a mill, there are some of the most interesting prehistoric markings, mainly spirals, on the 'Jack Rock'. At Warkworth (*Werceworthe* in 1150) the settlement was named after Werce, an abbess of Tynemouth in the seventh century. Amble, now a yacht marina, (*Ambell* in 1204) is Anna's promontory. Birling (*Berlinga* in 1187) may be one of the earliest names, commemorating the settlement of Baerla.

Further south is Hauxley, (*Hauekeslaw*), meaning either Hafoc or Hawk's mound, or perhaps a burial mound. This part of the coast has revealed a number of early Bronze Age burials. Druridge (*Dririg*) is a dry ridge, a name that fits in with its line of sand dunes, a place that has taken centre stage with protests against the removal of so much sand commercially, the upheaval of land for open cast coal mining, and against its becoming either a burial ground for nuclear waste or as the site of a nuclear power station. Much of the area close to the coast has been or is being mined and re-landscaped, and it will be interesting to see whether the restored fields have retained their names.

3

War and Peace:
the Border

One of the world's most dramatic frontiers is Hadrian's Wall, some of the most visually exciting parts of which are in Northumberland. The Wall is not the Anglo-Scottish border but was the line of demarcation between civilised Roman people and barbarians, known in the Vindolanda writing tablets as the Brittunculi.

Stretching from Wallsend in the east to the Solway, its forts, milecastles, turrets and ditches form links in a chain designed to control a frontier that in some ways put a brake on Roman Imperial ambition. The earlier Roman frontier, still there, was the Stanegate, a stone road, to the south of Hadrian's Wall. Vindolanda and Coria (Corbridge) lie upon it, serving as important supply bases and small towns. It is believed that Hadrian himself came to oversee the planning and building of the wall; it is fortunate for us that military considerations dictated that it should rise and fall with the whinstone scarps of the central section, leaving us with exhilarating scenery and walks as well as an interest in Roman achievement. Discussions about what it was for and how it operated go on. There are some common-sense points to be made. No one else at that time could possibly have built anything like it. It was a triumph of skill and organisation; the sheer size of it must have made the soldiers proud. Its building must have kept many soldiers busy with a strong sense of purpose.

The Wall has attracted archaeologists for many years, and it has been given its due through excavation, recording and publication. Our knowledge has received a boost through the activities of the Vindolanda Trust under the direction of Robin Birley and his wife, Pat and son, Andrew. Each year many new finds emerge, some of the greatest importance, some being the material culture of people who lived there, some being accounts in the writing tablets that give us further insight into their lives. There is considerably more to come from this complex multi-period site, much of it in the form of materials like leather, wood, metal, cloth and even human hair which the waterlogged conditions have preserved.

So attractive has this Roman frontier become that there is a national trail from Wallsend to Bowness-on-Solway, some 73 miles from coast to coast if it follows the line of the Wall exactly. There are some outstanding sites in Northumberland such as

The Roman Wall east of Cawfields.

Housesteads, Steel Rigg, Cawfields, Carvoran and Walltown Crags that are legally accessible and well displayed. The Whin Sill predominates: the great fault-line that includes vertically-cooled basalt forms a landscape of steep and undulating crags and small lakes, where there were people living in round huts before the Romans cut their military zone through the landscape. Perhaps they established small farms elsewhere; at Vindolanda the discovery of stone foundations of native-type huts suggests a theory that people living in round huts may have lived within the protection of the fort.

Elsewhere along the Wall there are little human touches, such as the soldier who carved his name and a phallus for good luck on a stone that he had quarried for wall building at Fallowfield or the decision by an anonymous group of soldiers who gave up the digging of the wall ditch through rock at misnamed 'Limestone Corner' where the basalt became too tough for them to quarry.

People in the past are elusive; we seldom find anything about their personalities. We can think of a tough band of soldiers, trained as ruthless killers, recruited from all over the Roman world, finding a place in the army with the possibility of citizenship at the end of it. In my frequent walks along the Wall I have tried to imagine them, only to come up with people rather similar to us. They were not on the whole from Rome, but they must have felt the cold and isolation of this foreign posting. I tried to capture the feeling of what it was like in this poem:

Hadrian's Wall. Housesteads

A place where empire halts.
Mist-haunted desolation holds in check
The will to move ahead.
And soldiers' eyes uneasily survey
Vast northern wastes;
An end to conquest, like a fire
That fades; but embers glow
And can be fanned into a flame.

A regiment of stone.
A geometric pattern coaxed from rock and soil,
Or forced persistently with toil.
Something to wonder at, admire;
Triumph of discipline
Ordering a landscape to obey.

Shut out the cold,
Stoke up the hypocaust,
Bring in our standards and our gods.
Each turret, fort and castle on the Wall
Becomes a reassurance of a different world.
The sound of marching, whiplash of command,
The clash of interlocking shields on alien soil;
Reaffirmation of the glory that is Rome.

Our hands rough-cut with mortar and sharp stone,
Legs stiff with pushing loaded carts through mud,
A finger broken on high scaffolding,
Thumb crushed by mauls in rock-cut ditch—
These were the lowest prices that we paid.
We joined the Legions, and we fought,
Became the masters of the north,
And our reward, as we are dwarfed,
Crushed in the shelter of our wall,
Housed in our barrack-blocks, patrolling roads,
Or dicing all our pay away
Is to be part of ranks on ranks of stone,
Cut to order, bound, by harsh winds flayed.

When I am dead
No one can really take my place.
This Wall will crumble, have to be rebuilt,

Fall down again, be quarried for its stone.
Yet I am part of it.
I lie in the foundations of a road,
Or feel the warm breath of calf in byre
Or watch a visitor admire the remnants of my work.

The story of the Roman frontier continues to be written and revised as new discoveries are made. The same is true of the story of the Anglo-Scottish border. What we see today is a frontier running from Berwick to the Solway Firth at such an oblique angle on the map that the northern parts of Northumberland are much further north than southern Scotland. Was it a frontier designed to keep people in or to keep them out? How was it decided? Did it appear at the stroke of a pen, or did it evolve? How do we know that we have crossed from one side to the other? Are the people on either side different from each other in speech, habits and outlook? If England and Scotland have different characteristics, does the Border mix them? Does the Border have a distinctive character?

The turn of the thirteenth century marked the beginning of one of the most violent periods in Northumberland's history. The fate of Hexham Priory in one of the earliest of the Scots' raids was shared by many other acts of desecration and destruction. But the violence was not one-sided, neither was it solely a matter between the English and the Scots, for the passing of armies across the border encouraged the law of the jungle in which there were hardly any rules except survival; neighbour raided neighbour.

The Scots

They poured along the valleys from the north
Like molten pitch, burning, destroying all before their way.
The Scots rampaged, a bloodlust veiled their eyes,
And they forgot the child they murdered could have been their own.
And they forgot despair of crops destroyed,
Of butchered kyle and slaughtered sheep,
For what they did was in a different world.
Damnation for their deeds returned in sleep.
For they would see the Priory burn,
The desecration of the cherished bones,
The beauty of creation broken down,
Destruction of the house of God,
Destruction of the people's town.

At their retreat they left a broken dream
And real lives lost to butchery and greed
A smoking heap of ruins laced with human bones.

Blood will have blood;
The English were to do the same
And back and forward armies marched
As people on the Borders caught the blast
Of hatred and of politics gone mad.

The nave became a graveyard for the town,
Bones piled on bones, covering Saint Wilfrid's crypt.
It waited centuries, for a more enlightened, peaceful age
To clear away the horror and renew the nave.
We are but dust, and must to dust return,
But we are the fire of inspiration that will burn
To recreate the town of Hexham and the House of God.

The Borders as an entity came into existence in the late thirteenth century when King Alexander III of Scotland broke his neck in 1286. Edward I of England pushed his own candidate John Baliol onto the Scottish Throne and began to interfere in the internal affairs of that country. Until then relations between the two countries had for the most part been reasonably happy. Religious Houses had been built on both sides of the border. There were some battles. From 1136–38 David had devastated Northumberland before his come-uppance at the Battle of the Standard at Northallerton. Then William the Lion invaded, and was captured at Alnwick by Henry II's men. In 1215 King John devastated both sides of the frontier in retaliation for Alexander II's support of the English barons opposed to him. Berwick, Alnwick and Morpeth were burned. The Scots retaliated, equally barbarously, but lost the northern Counties. This was followed by peace in which the 'national' border was established.

All this changed in the 1290s. Edward I's war to support his nominee followed a rigid plan of moving up the coastal plain, taking Berwick, where he slew thousands of people. He forced a Scottish submission five months later and left his minions in charge, thus winning the battles but losing the initiative. Scottish revenge followed. Wallace's victory at Stirling was followed by a devastation of Northumberland. Bannockburn saw the best-ever English army defeated by Robert Bruce in two days, and Bruce and Douglas once more devastated Northumberland.

The long-term effect of this vicious national rivalry was that the Borders became a buffer zone between conflicting national policies and forced the people to find ways to survive. They became Scots or English when it suited them, but their loyalty was to their '*Surnames*', a clan system that was complex because English and Scots could share the same surname across the Border. It was like the Mafia. There were deadly feuds in which neighbour would betray neighbour. Subsistence existence made it necessary to steal people's beasts and goods. With it came the rule of the jungle, a disrespect for human life. When the national armies marched through their territories they saw and experienced what these troops would do. They were spared no horror. We should not be surprised, when we have seen what happened in Rwanda, Bosnia and Kosovo. An army generates a cruel masculinity that shuts out pity and makes men forget what virtues they may have had at home. They have 'supped full of horrors'.

In this dog-eat-dog atmosphere what rules could possibly apply? The answer was: survival and expediency. Yet in 300 years of history would not people love or feel pity? Would they not crave for a peaceful world in which their children could grow up? Many sources of Border history concentrate on the lawlessness and violence. The name *Reivers* is given to the men of steel who bonded together and took what they wanted, be it animals, goods or people. It comes from the same root as 'bereft', that which is taken away. Some writers have expressed admiration for them because they were so clever in tactics and so tough and ruthless. Perhaps they have not used their imagination to place themselves in the position of the victims.

The places where raids took place vary. The coastal plain is gentle in its slopes and fertile; this was the main route taken by national armies. There are areas of high ground like the Cheviots with narrow valleys and bleak uplands that are inhospitable, infertile, but ideal for ambushes, raids, and for hiding stolen animals. Such areas have always suited nomadic people who herd and hunt. Sheep and cattle were the Borderers' chief wealth in such landscapes; transhumance meant that in summer they were taken onto high ground to pasture while the herdsmen based themselves in sheilings, temporary settlements for themselves and nightfolds for their animals. These sheilings could not be well protected, so far from more permanent settlements. Bishop Leslie, a Scot writing in the late sixteenth century says, 'They live chiefly on flesh, milk and boiled barley'. Meat, wool and skins were 'on the hoof' and could be captured and led off; it was essential to get them one way or another. As for cereal crops, oats, rye and barley could be grown, but standing crops could be burnt or removed. It was so difficult to plan.

There were six *Marches* designed as administrative units for the Borders. The English Middle March included most of the county, with the river valleys of Tynedale, Coquetdale and Redesdale. The north-east portion was the English East March from the Tweed to the Cheviots–Wooler–Alnwick line. Each unit had a Warden, and they were supposed to establish some sort of law and order, but the Wardens often had such a stake in the area and were linked to Reivers by family that they were anything but impartial in their judgements.

The coast was the route for armies; Berwick was of great importance, and here some of the worst atrocities were carried out. It ended up by being the most sophisticated of the northern fortresses in Elizabethan times, but by the time it was completed much of the international danger had receded. In the rest of the coastal belt many of the great castles of the men of power were situated.

In the Middle Marches Redesdale and Tynedale were the most troublesome areas, partly for reasons that become clear when you visit them today. They can be empty of people, remote, cold and not very productive, but full of sheep and cattle. This was ideal for those who wanted to raid unexpectedly and hide the results. There may have been a 'code' for the Borders, but when it came to the crunch, what were the rules and who was to enforce them? We are thinking here about thousands of people in the Border regions over a period of hundreds of years. In the absence of good government, which was not offered either by England or Scotland because it was in their interest to keep it seething, we have the 'Godfather' figures, the local heads of clans who in return for their protection of the people claimed services in return. This has come into our language as blackmail. They also use kidnapping and torture.

To appreciate the situation, this passage written by Sir Robert Bowes in 1550 on the state of the frontiers and Marches will help:

> If the thief be any great Surname or kindred and be lawfully executed by order of the Justice, the rest of his kin and surname bear as much malice which they call deadly feud against such as follow the law against their cousin the thief as though he had unlawfully killed him with a sword. And will by all means they can seek revenge there upon. And in times past they have in sundry times broken out of order the whole country. And they have then like rebels or outlaws committed very great and heinous attempts at burning or spoiling of whole townships and murdering the gentlemen and others whom they have grief or malice unto, so that for defence of them there have been great garrisons laid.

When the keepers of Tynedale and Redesdale are able to resist and pursue them, 'they will flee and keep themselves either in woods or mountains for their safety rather than they will be apprehended fly into Scotland and become outlaws and rebels'.

The Calendar of Border Papers contains this report in 1597 that shows how the most notable of the local lords were involved in raids:

> The 4 commissioners charge Sir Walter Scott laird of Buccleugh, Keeper of Liddesdale, with a hostile invasion of Tynedale on the 17th instant, where he cruelly murdered 35 of the Queen's subjects, sparing neither age nor sex, cutting some in pieces with his own hand, burning others, and drowning others—also burning 10 houses, and dividing the goods of the country among his own men, in reward for service.

This was done on a Sunday when he had been summoned to Carlisle for a Queen's commission because of his attack on Carlisle castle. They wanted the Scots authorities to support them in bringing him to justice. The people were terrified of him, and left their homes and summer sheilings. To counter this kind of attack, at least one hundred foot soldiers were needed from Berwick.

Did the Church have any influence on what was going on? Very little, it seems. A visitor to Liddesdale across the border saw no churches there and asked if there were any Christians. The reply was no; they were Elliotts or Armstrongs.

One of the most interesting documents is that in which the exasperated Archbishop of Glasgow calls down a public curse on the Reivers:

The piteous, lamentable and dolorous complaint comes to the ear of my Lord Archbishop of Glasgow how men, wives and bairns are murdered, slain, burnt, spoilt and reft, openly in daylight and under silence of the night, and their farms and lands laid waste by common traitors, reivers, thieves, dwelling in the south part of this Scottish realm, such as Teviotdale, Eskdale, Liddesdale, Nithsdale and Annandale. And therefore my said Lord Archbishop has thought expedient to strike them with the terrible sword of halykirk (holy church) and charges me to denounce, declare, and proclaim them openly and generally cursed at the market cross and at other public places: I denounce, proclaim and declare all and sundry the committers of the said murders, slaughters, burnings, kidnappings, reivings, thefts, spoilings with the GREAT CURSING.

I curse their head and all the hairs of their head; I curse their face, their een (eyes), their mouth, their naise, their tongue, their teeth, their shoulders, their breast, their heart, their stomach, their back, their arms, their legs, their hands, their feet, and every part of their body, frae the top of their head to the sole of their feet, before and behind, within and without.

I curse them gangang (going) and I curse them rydang; I curse then standand and I curse them sittand; I curse them eatand, I curse them drinkand; I curse them walkand, I curse them sleepand; I curse them at hame, I curse them fra hame; I curse them within the house, I curse them without the house; I curse their wives, their bairns, and their servants, their corns, their cattles, their wool, their sheep, their horse, their swine, their geese, their hens, and all their quick-good (all living goods). I curse their halls, their chambers, their kitchens, their barns, their byres, their cailyards, their ploughs, their harrows, and the goods and houses that is for their sustentation and welfare. And finally I condemn them perpetually to the deep pit of hell to remain with Lucifer and all his fellows, and their bodies to the gallows of the Burrow Mure.

Outsiders were resented. Long after the so-called peace, travellers still steered well clear of Housesteads Roman fort where the south gateway had been reused as a fortified tower by a lawless group who lived there. One thing that Borderers had in common was a resentment of outsiders. But one important unifying factor was that they intermarried, although this was forbidden by law because the authorities were anxious to keep the English and Scots separate; this suited their policy. There are stories that tell how the clans fancied each other's women and men. They shared a geographical entity. They probably shared a local speech, and were 'no cripples with their tongues.' They had clan loyalty and in some parts they had 'No Prince but a Percy', with a strong adherence to the lords who wielded such great power over their lives.

BORDERLINES

We have caught glimpses of life for the Border people, and it is the conditions in which they lived that produced a unique literary genre known as *The Border Ballads*.

There was a time when children encountered these ballads in anthologies that worthy academics thought fit for the young. As a boy, I found that odd lines remained with me for a while, but having to translate these verses did not help me to appreciate them. As stories, they seemed a bit odd, as some had no beginning and no end.

The full impact of Border Ballads came to me later in life, and particularly when James Reed read *The Ballad of Percy Reed* in the vernacular to a small group in Alnwick Castle. He and his students had come to Alnwick College of Education, marvellously housed in the castle, to study the setting of the Ballads, and my Main Course English students and I were about to take over a part of Bingley College so that we could investigate methods of teaching English as a second language in Bradford. His passion for this ballad was partly because it concerned his ancestors.

The Ballad of Percy Reed is from the English Middle Marches. Raiders from Liddesdale harried Redesdale and Percy Reed of Troughend took Crosier to the law. Crosier threatened him and his family with death. After a day's hunting Percy slept between the heather and the bent at Batinghope where the Halls of Redesdale, whom he trusted, poured water in his long gun and fixed his sword in the scabbard so that it wouldn't come out again. Four Crosiers appeared over the Hanging-stone, the Halls ran off, and Percy was left defenceless. They wounded him 33 times, hacked off his hands and feet, and left him there. He was found by a herdsman, who gave him a drink of water and agreed to carry the news to Percy's family. Questions, repetitions and responses thrust the narrative on.

Lamkin, associated with Nafferton Tower, east of Corbridge, is another story of treachery. Lamkin was a stonemason who claimed that he had not been paid for his work, so when the Lord was away he persuaded the nurse to let him into the tower where they attracted the lady of the house downstairs by jabbing the baby with a knife to make him cry. The lady appeared in her silks, and despite her pleas, Lamkin and the nurse ritually executed her, spilling her blood into a scoured basin. When the lord returned he found his wife and son murdered.

Many of the Ballads, like these, are based on purely local events, but with a universal theme.

There are exceptions such as *The Battle of Otterburn*. The Earl Douglas, the Earl of March and Dunbar and the Earl of Murray took Percy, Earl of Northumberland, by surprise with a raid that ravaged the country as far as Durham. Douglas returned with his booty to Newcastle, where skirmishing took place around the impregnable walls. Douglas captured Percy's pennon and taunted him with it, but the English remained in the safety of the walls. Douglas wanted to draw Percy into battle, which he did at Otterburn. By then Percy had realised that Douglas' force was only a small one and that the main Scottish army was at Carlisle. An English force, although outnumbering the Scots by about three to one was defeated in a moonlight battle; Douglas was killed and Percy was captured. The prophecy that 'a dead man should win the field' was fulfilled.

Violence is a frequent element, which is hardly surprising, whether the scale is a battle or an individual tragedy. What distinguishes the traditional, genuine Ballads from other narratives is that in telling the story there is no intention of giving us all the details. The stories were passed on as songs or by recitation originally. Thus they would have changed with the telling/singing. *The Twa Corbies*, again from the Middle March, is told as a conversation between two crows (or ravens) which are about to feast on the body of a dead knight who has been deserted:

> His hound is to the hunting gane
> His hawk to fetch the wild-fowl hame,
> His lady's ta'en another mate,
> So we may make our dinner sweet.

The plan is to pick out his lovely blue eyes and to take his golden hair to line their nest. No one knows where he is, so the wind will blow evermore over his white bones. The dialogue is dramatic and chilling. Questions lie unanswered—did his lady do this to him, and why? Who was he?

Another famous local Ballad is *Lord Randall*, where the driving force is question and answer. The repeated questions are 'Where?' and 'What?' asked by his mother. He is dying, and his mother concludes that he has been poisoned. Again there is betrayal; we can't be sure of the details, but he has been dining with his 'true-love'.

The Ballads fit into the historical and geographical background, and their sparseness of treatment gives them power. Those that are not based on documented or supposed historical events may involve the supernatural. *The Wife of Usher's Well* shows how the real world and the worlds of the supernatural co-exist. A wealthy woman loses her three sons at sea, but she invokes powers that bring back her sons from the dead 'in earthly flesh and blood'. We know that they are dead because 'their hats were o'the birk', a tree that grows in Paradise. And how does she greet them?

> Blow up the fire, my maidens!
> Bring water from the well!
> For a' my house shall feast this night,
> Since my three sons are well.

She treats their return from the dead as a normal occurrence, with the equivalent of 'Put on the kettle and make their beds,' but the cock crows and the chilling inevitability of the consequences of death are faced:

> The cock doth craw, the day doth daw,
> The channerin' worm doth chide;
> Gin we be mist and o' our place,
> A sair pain we maun bide.

The second line is a masterpiece! Many may have a revived interest in the Ballads through the music and singing of groups such as Steeleye Span and among local Folk groups. It is through singing them that the Ballads' impact is truly felt, but helps if people like James Reed read them aloud too. These verses were born in a region that is bleak, where one frequently comes face to face with death as an everyday reality, where people experienced all kinds of violence, and where ghosts and the living share the same land.

Finally, as mentioned before, there is a type of ballad that tells of an important event. *The Raid of the Reidswire*, a skirmish fought on the Anglo-Scottish border, commemorated at Carter Bar, began as a Wardens' meeting on 7 July 1575 to redress grievances and to present wrongdoers for a hearing. It attracted more than the Wardens and their representatives and became a big local event. The English had many Tynedale men among them, and the Armstrongs were well represented on the other side. Sir John Forster was the English Warden, one of the greatest rogues anywhere, and Sir John Carmichael, opposite in temperament and reputation represented the Scots side.

> I am accompted a negligent officer, an oppressor, a man more inclined to private gain and lucre, a destroyer and not a maintainer of the Borders, a bearer with the Scots and their actions, and a maintainer of them against my own countrymen.

He was worse than all this, but he added 'God forbid that any of them could be proved gainst me!' Ambiguous?

A bill was filed against a Robson of Falstone, who had wronged a Scot, but he hadn't turned up to answer the accusation and Forster made excuses. Carmichael more or less accused him of dishonesty, it grew heated and 'From wordis they fell to strokis'. The Tynedale men fired arrows, the Jedburgh men fought back, and there was a pitched battle in which the Scots came off best. Sir John was among the English taken prisoner to Edinburgh, embarrassingly for the Scots, and was returned to England. A Border commissioner could not apportion blame. The Ballad sings of these events, and ends:

> Who did invent that day of play,
> We need to not fear to find him soon;
> For Sir John Forster, I dare well say,
> Made us this noisome afternoon.

Apparently Sir John was to die at the age of 101.

DEFENSIVE TOWERS

The absence of secular buildings without defences in Northumberland from 1300–1550 emphasises the importance of defensive towers. Traces of the homes of people able to afford anything elaborate are rare. There are many castles of great size and importance, which leave a strong after-image with visitors, but there are or were hundreds of 'towers' with such different characteristics that the blanket term 'pele towers' is not very helpful.

There are two main types of tower: keep towers of at least three floors, and two storey bastles. The former were generally for the use of landowners, and the latter for tenants and staff, built in post- medieval times.

To appreciate this, it is interesting to visit a selection of the more accessible. One of the best preserved and most attractive is the 'Vicar's Pele' at Corbridge at the edge of the church graveyard, opening up onto the market place. Despite the obvious defensive nature of the tower there is consideration here for some comforts, such as light flooding through the thick walls and a good lavatory. The picture at *The Black Middens Bastle* is gloomier, for here we have one of a cluster of small bastles in the Gatehouse area with an external stone staircase in a bleak and remote region near Bellingham. These structures capture the atmosphere of the remote, empty spaces of the Border, where life was hard and an emphasis placed on the raising of animals that became the prey of raiding gangs.

Black Middens is open to the public: a simple block with an outside stone staircase, which replaced a wooden one, where the remains of curved roof supports still spring from the thick walls where they are embedded. There are slots for floor beams, part of the ground floor is covered with stone slabs, and there are small fireplaces. Outside is the ruin of another, later building, and the whole is surrounded with a low wall.

A survey of 1541 says that early structures had 'walls and roofs of squared oak trees bound together and mortised. The whole is covered with earth or turves so that they may not be set on fire and they are so strong that only with great force and numbers can they be cast down.' None survives, and none has been excavated.

The best of the surviving bastles is *Woodhouse*, at Holystone, which still stands to its full height and has an internal stair, so there was no need for an upper doorway. The ground floor has a tunnel vault. In the gable end is a ground floor doorway with a date stone 1602 WPBT TAM, the year before the accession of James I, after which life very slowly began to improve for the borderers. This was a very up-market bastle.

Aydon Castle (English Heritage), near Corbridge, is one of the best buildings to visit if you are looking for an illustration of the continuity of life on the Border, for it was established only a very short time before the long conflicts in the late thirteenth century. It was a 'hall house' that had no need of elaborate defences, but times changed: a defensive courtyard wall was built, a curtain wall and two towers. It has survived very well with continuing use as a farm, and now a centre for school parties and medieval 'events', probably because it changed hands without much of a fight.

Finally, a visit to *Preston Tower*, just off the A1 at Ellingham, is well worthwhile. It is a very small hall tower, originally built in the fourteenth century with four corner turrets, but now sliced in two. Later buildings clustered around it until in 1864 Henry Robert Baker-Cresswell restored it and inserted a large clock that he built. Major Tom Baker-Cresswell, who was chairman of the governors of one of my schools, and who belongs to the family once so intimately connected with Old Bewick, has made a visit to the tower a personal invitation to us to share with him his reflections on the life on the Borders. It is a fascinating place: a survival of old structures that gives an insight into history, the Ballads, and some local anecdotes, and into the visible working of a clock mechanism.

Aydon 'castle'; a fortified farm near Corbridge.

DECLARATION OF PEACE

In 1603 James VI of Scotland came to the English throne as James I, a very important moment for both countries. It did not mean that all suddenly became peaceful on the border, because the Commonwealth ushered in more strife, but it did give peace a chance. Conditions of life in Northumberland began to improve very slowly in a way that is reflected in the buildings; less emphasis was placed on defensive features and more on comfort and style. It enabled big landowners to exploit their estates more effectively.

There are many signs of this transformation, none more eloquent than at Belsay Castle, where one of the finest early tower houses was extended with the building of a two-storey Jacobean house by Thomas and Dorothy Middleton. This probably involved the redevelopment of old annexed buildings; the wall at the back of the tower has recycled late medieval masonry that indicates that the tower did not stand alone. The 1614 house still has a porch with its inscription to the Middletons, although it was remodelled in 1862. Further west are the remains of an eighteenth-century extension. Despite the additions and modifications, this area has a compelling medieval atmosphere, and the views from the roof of the tower are delightful.

The setting of this part of the estate, and the walk between it and the neo-classical box-like structure that was built between 1807–17 is one of the great delights of

Belsay castle: the west part (left) was added to the defensive tower when the land became more peaceful.

landscaping. Children especially love the old tower, and the winding paths through the maze of quarry gardens are intriguing, as well as providing some exotic plants. There is a contrast between the honey-coloured stone of the old tower and the darker, iron-spotted regular stone blocks of the soulless box conceived by Sir Charles Monk (who changed his name from Middleton in accordance with the demands of his maternal grandfather's will). The big empty spaces inside the house have found a new use as a centre for exhibitions. The area was developed in the nineteenth and twentieth centuries with parkland, terraces and lakes beautifully landscaped, and well maintained. Even so, visitors have to be reminded not to steal cuttings of plants and to keep clear of some of the most sensitive areas. If you like that kind of thing, or perhaps even understand what they are doing, a local croquet club dresses for the occasion on a green beside a path leading from the hall to the quarry gardens.

Chipchase makes a similar transition, but remains privately owned. The tower was begun in the mid-fourteenth century, and in 1621 the house was rebuilt and altered in Georgian times. An array of windows floods the building with light from the south, in contrast to the narrow slits of the tower.

At *Halton*, built south of the Roman fort of *Onnum*, the tower builders took advantage of the readily available source of Roman stones in the fourteenth century. The house was built on an older house site and linked to the east wall of the tower in the late seventeenth century. It is private, but can be appreciated from the outside, perhaps linked to a visit to the accessible building at Aydon, perched on the chasm of the Cor Burn.

Further west into the Borders is *Hesleyside*, power base of the Charltons, who acquired a classical mansion to replace a stone tower in a landscape set out by Capability Brown, who was born at *Kirkharle*.

At Ford and Chillingham castles changes were introduced a little earlier within the protection of their walls, with the addition, for example, at Ford of large windows to an Elizabethan range of buildings against the old north wall, and with the building of an elaborate entrance and inner courtyard at Chillingham.

On a smaller scale, the accessible *Blackbird Inn at Ponteland* shows many changes to an existing fortification. The sixteenth-century mullioned windows are built into earlier masonry, where the ground floor of the tower is tunnel-vaulted. This may have been part of a larger hall house. We are told on a carefully painted notice board outside that the building belonged to Mark Errington; his initials appear over a window, a door and the lintel of a fireplace, when he altered and extended the house in 1597. The information board draws attention to the vast numbers of children that he fathered.

These few examples show how buildings were adapted to the new era of peace, but the time came when prosperity from agriculture and industry brought in new wealth and the urge to display this wealth in building from scratch.

Existing power bases continued to be changed to suit the owners, *Alnwick Castle* being a splendid example. Here we have a moated keep standing between two baileys (wards), surrounded by walls pierced by one of the finest barbican entrances in Britain, with interval towers that show different periods of construction and renovation. As home to one of the most powerful of northern dukes, rising above the river Aln, with the town walls adjoining it, the castle was considerably modified to reach the habitable and oft-visited stately home that has been used often for film and television, including *Mary Queen of Scots*, *Elizabeth*, *A Yank in the Court of King Arthur*, the *Blackadder* series whose star was born in Stocksfield, and *Harry Potter*.

I was fortunate to help train students for teaching for 11 years when the castle was a College of Education, before the college closed in 1977. It meant that young and mature students brought not only income to the area, but gave to schools an opportunity to train future teachers. Many came to the area and stayed. Many local children, in distant rural areas and in the industrial towns such as Ashington and Lynemouth will, I hope, remember many of them with affection, for they brought with them a flavour of other places and skills. Since its closure, the Duke has welcomed students from Minnesota, and the ethos is different. A large building like this needs income, otherwise it goes the way of Warkworth or Prudhoe castles. The best way to preserve an old building is to use it, and Alnwick can still offer a place to train young people, a showpiece to visitors a stage-set for drama, and for the exciting development of the Alnwick Garden.

Small domestic buildings were raised in the seventeenth century in more peaceful times; this had not been possible before, because of war. There were not many people

Chipchase castle, with the early tower to the left.

Halton: largely built of Roman stone, a more elegant wing was added when the danger of attack receded.

and no sudden wealth, so the process of building houses in the country was slow. The new houses do not show much variety in style, but they are built in stone and of good quality. Thatch was used on many roofs, still evident in old photographs, made of heather or straw. Thin, easily split sandstone provided roofing and flagstones, especially in the south. Slate was imported, but local clays also provided good tiles. Sandstone was the ubiquitous building material, with the addition of dolerite in places where the Whin Sill threaded through the landscape. Whinstone is a fine-grained igneous rock that, when it was molten, flowed over existing sedimentary rocks and crystallised into vertical columns. It is prominent in the central section of the Roman Wall and at Bamburgh, Dunstanburgh and the Farne Islands. It has been difficult to use as ashlar facing because it is so hard to shape, but it made good packing between sandstone blocks on the Wall and in castle walls like Dunstanburgh. Today it provides tough road metal.

Brick was hardly used before the nineteenth century, with exceptions such as Dorothy Forster's house in Alnwick. It was not until the growth of the coal industry with its subsidiary works that bricks became the favourite building material in urban areas. One brick-works outside such areas is off the A697 near the Alnwick-Rothbury crossroad. Known as the Swarland Brick Works it takes advantage of a very thick clay deposit brought down in the Ice Ages, and although the bricks became gas-fired, little else has changed, except that the site has been mothballed for a while, and a fire has broken out.

The rebuilding programme in the country did not come until the early nineteenth century, in which most of the farmhouses were rebuilt, and as we see at Old Bewick, there was a movement among farmers and landowners to improve their workers' cottages.

In some areas villages were 'planned', after the old settlements were deliberately destroyed and their sites re-used. At *Ford* the old village round the tower and west of the church and castle was swept away to open up the view across the Milfield Plain to the Cheviots, and a new village was built to the east.

At *Haughton*, a hall house (called a 'castle') near Hexham, the village was demolished, leaving a fragmentary medieval chapel standing forlornly in a field.

At *Blanchland* the old Abbey courtyard was developed as a new village by the Lord Crewe Estates. Like Haughton, its potential has been realised by filmmakers. *Belsay*, *Cambo* and *Chillingham* are all planned villages, the Cambo old post office being a modified fortified tower. The influence of rich landowners is seen in estate houses bearing their insignia. Perhaps the most interesting rural development that brings us closer to our time is at Swarland, where the village was laid out before the Second World War to house homeless Tyneside families.

Buildings reflect what materials are available or what is fashionable to import. They reflect wealth, social aspiration and fashion. In Northumberland the landed estates were vast, with about half the county occupied by them in 1873. The power of the landlords was used to improve agriculture, create wealth and to invest that wealth in new industries based on coal. What we see today is largely the result of their policies, in both town and country. Trees and hedges were planted in their

Haughton 'castle' is a fortified hallhouse.

Wallington dragons' heads, brought from Bishopsgate.

thousands, fields with straight boundaries were created and roads were built. The Blackett family, for example, made fortunes out of coal and lead, bought the Fenwick estates, and rebuilt *Wallington* and *Paines Bridge*. As we shall see, *Ford* was developed by the Delavals. The Swinburnes developed much of north Tynedale. Above everyone in importance were the Dukes of Northumberland, whose estates remain well ordered, attractive and profitable.

4

A Microcosm:
Ford, Etal, Flodden

Ford Castle, as its name implies, was built to control a major fording place on the River Till. Set on a sandstone ridge, it overlooks the Milfield Plain, a large dried-up glacial lake filled with sand, gravel and clay deposited by water and ice sheets. The plain or basin attracted settlement and ritual enclosures in prehistoric times, and because it was fertile and well drained in many parts it continued to be of importance, There are small Saxon houses and a large wooden palace known as *Maelmin* similar to that excavated at Yeavering, visible only from the air and under the right conditions. Important routes lead into it; from the south at Wooler ('the margin of the water') is the Haugh, where the Wooler Water divides the volcanic Cheviot rocks from the sandstone scarp to the east, leaving a strip of flat land where the English army camped before moving to fight the Scots at Flodden. The plain is joined by the Till from the east, where the river makes a sharp turn to break through the sandstone ridge at *Weetwood Bridge*, and by the Glen from the west. All flow together as one major tributary of the Tweed. At *Doddington* and *Roughting Linn*, both important prehistoric sites, streams flow to the Till, and prehistoric motifs sign the land where these routes lead to prehistoric ritual sites of lines of pits, enclosures and henges under the soil.

Ford started its life as a manor house of some sort with a spiral staircase now incorporated in one of the four linked towers, the result of the king's giving Sir William Heron permission to 'crenellate' it in 1338. The date is well into the period of Anglo-Scottish wars. Not far away *Etal* and *Chillingham* were built on a similar quadrilateral plan. Ford and Chillingham are still lived in.

Ford owes its appearance to the fortunes and characteristics of the people who have owned it, and represents a microcosm of county history. Since 1907 it has been owned by the Joicey family, but is leased to Northumberland County Council and used as a residential centre that has given to hundreds of young people and adults the chance to live there and to learn from the environment. It is a rare resource that concentrated its energies on teaching people to think for themselves and to learn from direct experience. Unfortunately the cost-cutting exercise by the County Council, forced on it by the government financial policy led to its

Ford castle in 2013, the front.

closure recently. One of the best ways to preserve old buildings like this is to use them.

The layout of the buildings and the variety of stonework tell their own complex story to those trained to look carefully. Of the four towers two have largely original stonework. The James Tower, so named because King James IV of Scotland is said to have spent his last night there before the battle of Flodden, is supported by a ribbed vault, the walls rising above it being thick enough to contain a staircase. Of course this became known as a secret stair that connected James' room to that of Lady Heron, whose husband was a prisoner in Scotland. Generations of children, and adults, who have worked and slept there have passed on stories of ghosts, and of prisoners confined to black dungeons. It is what is expected of an old building. The discovery of a walled-up painting several years ago created a stir and raised the possibility that this was the young wife of an old Delaval who, after his death, was forbidden access to most of the rooms, but the periods do not match. Even so, who was she and why was the picture hidden?

The James Tower, considerably restored, is a formidable structure. The main room (the 'study') is one of five storeys. It has wide modern windows to let in light, splayed through the thickness of the walls, on to a thick-planked floor. Around the walls were reminders of the origin of the castle in a replica Licence to Crenellate, replicas of some of James' possessions connected directly with Flodden, his portrait, and an Elizabethan fireback. Some moving programmes have been produced at the end of summer art and history courses in this room, in which members contributed in readings, drama, songs and instrumental music. On some occasions a lone piper has sat in the window space and played the Northumbrian pipes for all that wished to hear him before supper. It is a place that means different things to many people. James might have seen his army to the west on Encampment Hill as they waited for the English, but we know nothing of his thoughts on the night of 8 September 1513.

The tower is linked to a smaller one at the south-west by a curtain wall, of which some of the original masonry survives. The Cow or Flag tower has lovely irregularly-shaped blocks of stone built on a plinth set on outcrop, with a variety of colours as the wall rises. There are blocked openings and inserted windows and doors, and a place in the east tower wall from which the south wall ran. Between the two towers in the field that once housed the villagers and still has a 'vicar's pele' and the ridges of their field systems, a hollow way leads to the ford, and is probably the site of the original entrance.

The other towers were on the east, but the site of the south-east tower is now marked by a raised platform in the grass. The north-east tower has been completely rebuilt but is entered by an original newel staircase that must have been built for people who usually fought with their swords in their left hands. The Carrs, who once owned Ford, were carr-handed (or cack-handed elsewhere). Could there be a connection?

What we see today was largely reconstructed by the Delaval family, following the lines of an Elizabethan building with an E-shaped hall. Sir John Delaval was responsible for the 'Strawberry Hill Gothic' style that greets us at the southern gate, with its decorative portcullis. After 1761 the house was given arched windows and the forecourt was built with walls, parapets and the two clock towers and interval towers well beyond the limits of the original quadrangular castle. The buildings were further modified by Louisa, Marchioness of Waterford whose husband was a descendant of the Delavals and whose initials appear at frequent intervals around the castle.

The Delaval family had been prominent in Northumberland from Medieval times, but by the early eighteenth century their fortunes were rapidly declining until they were rescued by Admiral George Delaval who invested the considerable profits of his naval career in commissioning Sir John Vanbrugh to build a magnificent new hall at Seaton Delaval. His nephew, Francis, inherited the Seaton Delaval properties and also, from his mother, the Ford estates. Landowners in south-east Northumberland were just beginning to exploit the massive mineral wealth which underlay their estates and all should have been well for the family fortunes but Francis' son, another Francis, was determined to spend money more quickly than it accrued. He was famous in London society for his spendthrift ways. His love affairs were notorious and while he was in funds, he was generous to his mistresses. He had a fascination for the theatre and financed lavish performances including one of *Othello* at Drury Lane which was so famous that Parliament adjourned two hours early to see it. Many of the family were also involved and they became known as the 'Gay Delavals' (in the original sense of the word). They were notorious practical jokers and held wild parties at Seaton Delaval where the scandalous goings on became legendary in the district. Finally, Francis was made bankrupt and his brother, John, made trustee of the estates. John was an efficient businessman who fully exploited the riches of the mineral seams under his estates and developed the port of Seaton Sluice by making a new deep-water dock for the shipment of coal. With his brother Thomas, he built a bottle works which produced up to 10,000 bottles a month. John invested some of this wealth in the renovations at Ford and when he died, left the castle to his granddaughter, Susanna, wife of the Marquis of Waterford.

A strange story is attached to these eighteenth-century Delavals. When Francis inherited Ford and joined it to the Delaval estates, he placed a Ram's Head, the Delaval crest, above the door. Legend has it that the head spoke, predicting that while the two estates were joined, no male Delaval would die in bed. This certainly seemed to be the case; Francis the elder died after falling down the steps at Seaton Delaval and his son Francis perished from a surfeit of venison. Francis' brothers died in a variety of circumstances including two killed in action, one drowned and one blown up in an earthquake in Lisbon! John's son died aged 19 in an unfortunate incident reputedly precipitated by his over-amorous approaches to a serving maid while convalescing at Bath. Even John himself, the sensible hard-headed business-man lost control of his financial empire, took on a teenage mistress and died at the breakfast table. Only when the estates separated, Ford to the descendants of John's favourite daughter and Seaton Delaval entailed to another branch of the family, were the male Delavals allowed to die peacefully in bed.

Although in no way rivalling the riches of the south—east Northumberland coalfields, the Ford estate had its own small colliery, which is a good example of

The abandoned Ford Moss colliery village.

a typical small-scale rural operation, its products destined for local consumption.

At *Ford Moss*, now a designated area of outstanding botanical interest, coal had been extracted since the seventeenth century until the closure of the mine in 1914. It began with the digging of bell pits, circular shallow shafts with a collar of upcast around them; they follow the seams from above ground. What we see today are the remains of shafts, marked in some cases by circles of railway sleepers, a brick and stone chimney that provided power for pumping operations and for access to the underground seams, and the piles of slag that came from the furnaces. There is an isolated engine house, looking like a defensive tower, reached by an abandoned wagonway. Piles of shale and dark soil have become rabbit warrens, near the wood that hides a prehistoric enclosure. A ridge to the south has an abandoned freestone quarry with a rusting hoist still lying there. This could have been the source of the stone for the buildings essential to mining and for houses, school and chapel that were once there. The foundations of one small row of terraces (known as 'Blue Row') and the street are still there, and so are the rectangular allotments, with hedgerows of hawthorn, on their boundaries. A second row, just inside some bushes and scrub, has well-cut stone fireplaces. In all there are signs of about thirty houses. Molehills and rabbit holes turn up glass fragments and pottery sherds, and on one occasion a doll's terracotta head, and these fragments are of interest to parties of young people who investigate the area. One derelict garden dutifully produces a crop of rhubarb each year. It is a place where nature is reclaiming its own. Slag heaps and other waste mounds are decorated with broom, birds flock in, and what remains of structures becomes overgrown. What it covers up is the life of generations of miners, many of them from outside the area, who with their families established an industrial community. We do not know much about how they related to other local people. The mine could not compete with other coalfields, and the problem of water seeping into the workings became so acute that at one stage everyone had to abandon the mine, leaving all their tools behind them. We find that High School groups respond particularly well to this location, both in scientific observation, reporting and in creative writing.

In contrast to this late episode in human history, the ridge that rises to the south and overlooks the Broomridge valley and the sea in the other direction, has panels of prehistoric rock art, the sites of destroyed cairns, and a rise in the rocks to the east at Goatscrag Hill where the rock overhangs have early Bronze Age urned burials in the floors and a panel of four deer on one vertical surface. As in so many places, the use of the landscape is not limited to a single period, as there are also the outlines of millstones and circular depressions from which they have been taken on one outcrop, and the whole area has been rig and furrow ploughed, thus disturbing any surface archaeology. Trees have been planted on the ridge slopes, but at *Dove Crags* fantastic shapes of eroded sandstone cliffs occupy spaces between plantings and they fascinate artists.

After a number of small local TV and radio programmes on various aspects of prehistory, I was asked in 1998 to do a programme with BBC2 as part of their *The Essential Guide to Rocks*; I was to explore with Ray Mears some locations of rock art. Three areas were chosen: Weetwood, Dod Law and Broomridge, all on the sandstone scarpland overlooking the Milfield Plain, all with impressive panels of decorated stone on outcrop rock and all with a connection with prehistoric burial sites. The Broomridge location included the making of a cup and ring motif; Ray carried a small sandstone slab to the top of the ridge and, with a naturally-pointed piece of andesite that we found in the River Glen, he used it as a hand pick rather than with a mallet to chip the design into the rock. As the sandstone was fairly soft, it did not take long. The episode was filmed in strong winter sunshine close to decorated outcrop with splendid views in all directions—like being on top of the world—and this newly made cup and ring was laid next to the 5000 year old ones, water from shallow pools was added, reflecting the sunlight and increasing the contrast, and filming was accompanied by an unexpected reverence and silence. The place and the activity got to us all.

Ray Mears was fascinated by this ridge, and when I took him to see the images of four deer on the vertical interior of a rock overhang he at once related them to others that he had seen abroad in 'ancient' settings. One has bent legs and is running; the others are static. When I told him that flints and two inverted burial urns had been excavated on the rock shelter floor where he was standing, with the enormous view to the south flooded with low light, we became involved in such an animated discussion about the significance of 'special' places that the director had to call us to heel to get on with the filming.

The ridge drops to a steep stream valley, and at a place where two streams join is the entrance to a narrow valley that leads to a small waterfall called *Roughting Linn*. The valley creates a powerful atmosphere of mystery, with occasional shafts of light breaking through and the silence broken by the noise of falling water. The name means that the water bellows like a bull into the pond. It is only a small waterfall, but in its setting it is hypnotic. I have led many children and adults down the stream valley slope into this place, but one of the most memorable descents was when a long-retired Ashington miner who had become well-known for his paintings asked us to take him down there, come hell or high water. We did so with the help of a strong rope lashed to a tree. His delight with the place justified his determination, for this valley narrows into steep-sided small sandstone cliffs with layers like wafers and pock-marked with small holes. There is a rock overhang. The water drops from a small ledge into a pond that I suspect may have been used for offerings by the people who lived enclosed by arcs of ditches and earth walls that reach the edge of this valley. Don't expect anything large scale, but expect to enter a strange and powerful world, 'holy and enchanted'.

The BBC missed this place as we moved to the famous rock art panel further east: a 60 foot (18 m) whaleback of sandstone shaped like a great elongated burial mound, covered with symbols. It is the largest outcrop of decorated rock in England, partly quarried away before Canon Greenwell discovered it about 150 years ago. It poses many questions about how rock art should be displayed; an English Heritage Pilot Project, in which I was involved, published a large report that is a very useful blueprint for future work, and the poor display at Roughting Linn, uncertainty

Broomridge: west from Goatscrag Hill to the Milfield Plain.

Roughting Linn waterfall.

about how much damage tree roots and other growths are doing to the rock, and how it should be signposted and presented made it a test case. It is a fantastic place, though, shut in by trees and shrubs, and lying on a route that leads to Clive Waddington's Coupland 'henge' (older than Stonehenge) or cattle enclosure on the Milfield Plain from the coast. Northumberland remains one of the most important areas of prehistoric rock art in the world. Broomridge takes us deeply into a past from Neolithic to Iron Age, to millstone quarrying and to the mining of stone and coal.

To return to more recent times and to the village of Ford, it is easy to forget how self-supporting villages were, and how many diverse trades were followed. Local coal provided most houses in Northumberland with a cheap and easily accessible source of heat, and in some places there was peat. 'Directories' reveal a great range of skills and facilities. Children in Ford were educated in the nineteenth century in a very up-market school, and were surrounded by paintings on the walls of biblical scenes that included people that they knew as some of the Old Testament characters. The church was kept in good order partly by the estate owner's money and the vicar depended upon his or her patronage. Now villages struggle to keep their schools going or to retain their churches, post offices and banks. Change is part of history rather than 'progress'; it is about adapting to changed circumstances. The rig and furrow system of ploughing and land allotment seen in and around Ford is a sign of the change from arable to animal husbandry on a bigger scale. More sheep mean fewer people, and so do more sophisticated machines. Where there is no work the exodus to towns gathers momentum, especially when small local industries fail.

The Heritage industry, such as we see at Ford and Etal, flourishes in an age of increasing leisure, especially among the ageing population. Etal castle is one of the latest to have a centre, housed in the former Presbyterian chapel and manse, built *c.* 1750 and rebuilt in 1800. Branch railways may have closed, but the miniature passenger railway that takes people from *Heatherslaw Mill* to Etal through a swathe of wildflowers has proved very successful. Thank God that this is done tastefully, and that we don't have Mickey Mouse conducting tours of Border castles!

Ford and Etal are often called 'model villages'. At Etal Lord Joicey lives in a Georgian house set in a fine garden, with a chapel built in 1858. From here the street runs to the gatehouse of the castle and veers to the ford, where the remains of a water mill are still visible. The thatch used on some of the buildings is a reminder that this was a common material, but a fairly recent fire caused roofing materials to be replaced is another reminder of its dangers. Others have large heavy slates, topping the white-painted walls. Unlike Ford, Etal has a village pub. Most of the buildings are replacements ordered by Lord Joicey after 1907, when he bought the estate.

Ford village replaced an older one that shared the same field as the 'Parson's tower'. What the people who lived in the old houses thought of this enforced move we are not told. After 1860 a straight street was laid out from the granite column, 1859, commemorating the Marquis of Waterford, to the east to 'Jubilee Cottage', complete with Queen Victoria's bust. The Waterford houses, well spaced out, are on a smaller scale than the later Joicey Cottages (with their dates inscribed), but the building that catches the eye is the Waterford Hall. This elaborate Victorian

Roughting Linn rock art on a large whaleback of outcrop sandstone.

Etal settlement, ancient and modern.

Tudor-type school has its attractive patterned deep blue and green slated roof over steep gables; the family crest dominates. At the top of the street to the left is the unusual front of the blacksmith's shop, dated to 1863; its door surround is a large sandstone horseshoe. The wall leading to the farm and more estate houses is unusual, with its large chunky capping stones.

The church of St Michael and All Angels is earlier than the castle; built in the thirteenth century; it has been over-restored. Its most impressive external feature is the bellcote, standing like a chimney with its lancets capped by a pyramid of stone. The sandstone in this tower has a beautiful range of colour and texture. Inside the church is the thirteenth-century grave slab of a bagpiper, very important, if not unique in Britain. The bagpipes portrayed here and on the tomb of Prior Leschman in Hexham Abbey are of the Scottish and Breton type. Air is blown into a bag by mouth. In Chaucer's day the Canterbury Pilgrims were led by the Miller, an uncouth and unpleasant man who was well fitted to play an uncouth instrument that has since changed its image.

For me, one of Ford's main associations is with Kathryn Tickell who came to the castle with Carol and Anthony Robb many years ago to play for our adult courses in art and history. She was a young teenager, absorbed by her art as she played fiddle and Northumbrian pipes, and so great was her talent that it was easy to predict a great future for her. She has taken her art to great heights. Her fame is now international, but her roots remain in Northumberland, especially in Wark, in the Wanney hills, and at Rothbury. Her family and other instrumentalists were her inspiration, but so is the landscape. Others draw inspiration from the same places: much of Gordon Highmoor's painting is inspired by the remote landscapes around West Woodburn.

The River Till was not merely a barrier to be crossed; it was a source of power that the Delavals utilised. Today the most outstanding example of its use is the working mill at Heatherslaw, open to the public, and available for guided tours for school groups. Most of it is nineteenth century; the wheels are visible, the process of gears, grinding and bagging are clearly displayed, and the history of milling set out with 'hands-on' experience of grain rubbers and rotary querns used from prehistoric times onward. It is not just a place to learn. There are some homemade refreshments and the opportunity just to sit and watch the river rush by.

It is pleasant for visitors to share this landscape and its buildings, but that is only part of it, for the life of the significant soil goes on; crops, animals, buildings and landscape are still being managed. Gravel extraction continues on the Milfield Plain. Look further back, and the pretty picture dissolves, for life in this area would have been ghastly for many people.

Left and below: A grave slab in
Ford church and a bagpiper in
Hexham Abbey.

THE BATTLE OF FLODDEN

The James Tower at Ford may have gathered together and absorbed the laughter of thousands of children, but it is also a grim reminder of Flodden. From here James may have been able to see his troops across the plain on Encampment Hill, now planted with a line of trees running towards its summit. It was the largest army that Scotland had assembled at Edinburgh at the start of the invasion of England, but by then about 30,000 strong, somewhat depleted by those who went home to look after their farms or whatever. So far that army had had it all its own way, with little resistance to the capture of Norham, Wark, Duddo, Etal and Ford. They were rested, their huge cannon and smaller artillery supplied by their French allies were well positioned to beat off an English attack from the direction of Wooler. Into the valley of death? No, thank you; the Earl of Surrey had other ideas. Encampment Hill had been fortified before, by an Iron Age enclosure on its summit. It extended to Branxton Ridge, and then down to the fording places over the River Tweed. From there the Scots could see home.

James had certainly taken his 'yard of English soil' as requested by the French queen and was supported by their money and military advisers. But what was his strategy? Henry VIII's army was fighting in France, and England's backdoor was left open for the Scots to take advantage of a supposed weakness. But what

Flodden ridge from Ford churchyard.

was the point of the campaign? Where was this huge army going? Nowhere, it seems, despite encouraging successes. The great castle of Norham, in a detached part of the Bishop of Durham's territory, ran out of gunpowder and surrendered. The banner of St Cuthbert had not yet arrived with an English army. A strike further south was presumably ruled out. When the Earl of Surrey and his sons moved north to counter this invasion, the English plans had been well advanced for mustering the northern troops. They moved from Newcastle to Alnwick, and on to Wooler, where the impregnable nature of the Scottish position called for some deep thinking. James probably made decisions himself, but he was no strategist. It is important for a commander to gather information on which to act, and Surrey's next move was bewildering. He headed off with his army to Weetwood Bridge, then on to Bar Moor via Doddington. How could this be interpreted? One explanation that might have occurred to James was that he was aiming at Berwick, from where he could move towards Edinburgh. The battle had been fixed in response to Surrey's challenge for 9 September, and James had agreed to wait for him in a place of his choosing. Instead, Surrey and his men, low on provisions and out of beer, settled down for a short night at Barmoor on 8 September in the rain. It had been raining for most of the Scottish campaign, and one can imagine the state of the poor roads and especially appreciate the difficulty of moving artillery. (One large Scots cannon needed 36 oxen to move it, and a team of men to accompany it). So there we have an army of thousands camped east of Ford on fairly even ground, and another, larger army dug into positions on a hill to the west. The seventy-year-old Surrey took the risk of splitting his force of about 20,000 men, and sent his son Howard to outflank the Scots. He knew that he could not let this army escape to Scotland, where it would remain a constant threat in the future to England. If there were to be a battle, he would choose the spot, not James. They crossed the River Till at the fords and Twizell Bridge, which still stands, marched between Branxton ridge and the Tweed, and appeared on the Scots' western flank. Surrey followed with the rest of the army across the fords to face the Scots head on, with his own battle stationed at what is now called Piper's Hill.

Battles are not fought neatly, with nice blocks of troops and arrows marked on the map. Neither are they confined to one place. This one extended across about a mile of land, with Branxton Hill to the south dictating the movement of the Scots as they abandoned their position on the hill; they moved west, with the intention of then turning north to the Tweed valley. The rain was pouring down, and the mist was thickened by the smoke from the abandoned Scots camp. How much intelligence James had of the English move is not known, but he was forced to face the tactical reality of an English army appearing on his west flank. This initial attack was at first countered by Lord Home, and the English were routed and forced to join the main army to the east, but then followed an extraordinary act that was to affect the whole course of the battle: Lord Home continued down the hill to the Tweed and took no part in the rest of the battle. Whether he was doing what he was commanded to do, to hold the fords for the passage of the army, or

Flodden: Piper's Hill from Branxton churchyard.

whether his victory gave him the right to leave the rest to someone else, we shall never know. He later became a scapegoat for the failure and was executed. He left the flank of the Scottish army unprotected, and this allowed Dacre's Cumbrian cavalry to fill the gap and to complete a pincer movement. On the other flank were Stanley's Lancashire bowmen, prepared to fire their lethal swathes of arrows from longbows into the poorly-clad Highlanders commanded by Argyll and Lennox, with their French advisers.

The Howard family drew up their line of battle to face Crawford and James at the centre. There was the preliminary of an artillery barrage from both sides, in which the English proved more effective partly because the Scots guns were firing awkwardly downhill. The Scots position was fine at the top of Branxton Hill, where they looked down on the English, but the wet slope and some of their weapons—18 feet (5.5 m) long pikes unsuited to this kind of fight—were an encumbrance when they faced the English billhook. For this was the most bloody hand to hand fighting. James, with more bravery than sense led his army down the slope and almost reached Surrey. He was slain.

The outcome was not clear at first, as the Scots fought on in a hopeless position, and it was only the following morning when he reviewed the battlefield that Surrey knew that he had won. No one on the Scots' side was to write a ballad about this. 'The Flowers of the Forest' was a lament for Flodden written much later, and is a heart-wrenching response to the futile destruction of so many. It is estimated that

6–10,000 Scots were slain, including an archbishop and three bishops. The English lost about 1,500.

The Piper Hill memorial cross is inscribed to the brave of both nations. In August a lone piper stands there to play a lament before scores of people on horses ride up Branxton Hill to a less potent tribute. This is a place of great sorrow. Whether it would appear so unless we knew that a bloody battle had taken place is another matter.

From the cross, most of the Scots' positions can be seen, and in the other direction are the ridges and the Pallinsburn over which the English dragged their equipment to take up their positions. The church, with some Norman features, is restored, and there may be many dead buried there. The name Flodden only appears in 1513; it means a hill with a stream running by.

With our knowledge of what happened, Flodden can be an unbearable place. One thinks of all the people caught up enthusiastically in warfare, and for what? Adventure? Gain? A change of place? Loyalty to one's lords? Once in battle, the whole thing would have been total confusion and a matter of kill or be killed. For those who want to make it a matter of nationality, they rejoice or are sad according to which nation they support, but for anyone who looks more deeply into history to see the vanity, the power-seeking of those whose policies were followed, there can be no victors. The common people are mostly the losers. I am reminded of that extraordinary tower at Smailholm where Sir Walter Scott the novelist and poet was brought up; here is the very centre of Border legend, but the reality is that in such a small household three men were to die on the Scots side at Flodden. Places do have the power to move by their settings and by what happened there. They have the power also to make us think about our history, and cast away the romantic nonsense and flag-waving that often accompany it. It could be that after the battle the Borderers, like carrion, would have awaited their chance to move in on the wounded and the dead to take what was left. It was a world that they, of all people, would have understood, for violent death was part of life around them. For those who lost husbands and sons, the lament says it all:

> We'll hear no more lilting at our ewe-milking,
> Women and bairns are sad and wae;
> Sighing and moaning on this green loaning,
> The flowers of the forest have all faded away.

MONUMENTS

The monument on Piper's Hill is a plain, massive granite cross; there are no frills, no sentimentality. Monuments are designed to capture and store meaning, and the country is rich in them; grave stones, war memorials, statues and some buildings spring to mind. A megalith not far from Flodden to the east of the A697, although prehistoric, has been given a more recent function as *The King's Stone* by being

Above and right: Smailholm
tower on the Scots' side of the
Border, from a distance and
close up.

Duddo stones, erected *c.* 4,000 years ago.

linked in some way to the battle. Not so that most eloquent of all Neolithic/early Bronze Age stone circles at *Duddo*.

In a field that is almost constantly under the plough, on private land, a small circle of stones lies on the crest of a slight rise that has views of the Eildon Hills and the whole of the Tweed valley on the Scottish side, and the range of the Cheviot Hills in Northumberland. We know little about its history, except that someone who dug inexpertly in the centre reported finding a cremation. It is likely to be the burial place of some important person, displayed prominently so that it can be visited. The stones, deeply embedded, are mostly fluted with weathering, and at the base they are shaped so much like waists that one of the local names for them is 'The Women'. Another name is 'The Singing Stones', because somewhere the story spread that when the wind blows into the fluted stones they become musical. Be that as it may, the shapes and the way they face inwards with the vast landscape around them gives them tremendous character. By analogy we may assume a date for their erection of up to 5,000 years ago. No one has yet located their source, although fluting on cliffs and scarp edges is not unusual in local sandstone. Many claim them as their own, including Druids, although compared with the people who erected the stones, Druids are newcomers.

This is one of my reactions to the site:

Solstice: Duddo

On such a night the hills dissolved
And re-assembled in a shifting mist,
Numb with moonlight's touch.
We learnt that silence was not hostile,
Took upon ourselves its deepest strength
Waiting for dawn's layered sun.
A moon that paced
As crow's shout cracked the sky
Fled from the triggered bird-song
Hesitant, then loud.
Before our eyes, a second birth,
A new-created universe,
Green and blue and gold.
Fluted stones whose shapes had shifted
With emitted heat
From bearded barley heads,
Buried to the hips,
Reclaimed their circle and identity,
Introspective, Janus-headed,
Guarding and inviting
As the sun's diurnal course
Played a slow game
With shadow shapes
Time and time and time again.

5

The Tyne Valley

The approach to Hexham along the Tyne valley from the east begins with the plumes of smoke from the Egger factory. Here the trees felled in the uniform forests of conifers that now cover much of the county are pulped into chipboard. Industry continues west along the Tyne, joining with retail premises and car parks to cover land once devoted to market gardens and orchards. Floods in 1771 and 1782 swept away all the Tyne bridges except Corbridge, and the present bridge at Hexham was built in 1793; it is an attractive approach followed by the smaller hump of a railway bridge. The station, still in use, is surrounded by garages, indicative of the change from public to private transport. From the Wentworth Leisure Centre and its sports track the land rises to a bluff that is topped by some prominent old buildings—Gaol, Moot Hall and Abbey, almost rivalled in size but not in beauty by the brick wall of the Forum Cinema. A riverbank walk, with a boating house, playground, picnic area and golf course is tree-lined. The river has resident ducks that feed on visitors' bread, gulls that fight for scraps, the dignity and menace of herons, and a variety of other birds.

The wide river is now to some extent controlled by the Kielder reservoir; it swirls around the denuded piles of rail bridges that once carried branch lines, catching floating debris. The walk is popular all year round, and the river attracts canoeists and rowers. The re-sited Mart echoes with the plaintive sounds of beasts on market days.

It is clear from the river bridge approach that the town stands on a terrace above the haughs in the valley. Any hole dug in the ground there gives a cross-section of sand, rounded cobbles and clay, deposited by ice and water. Tributary streams cut through the terrace to the Tyne: the Cockshaw Burn and Cowgarth or Hallgarth Burn run through the town, and the Skinners Burn has been culverted.

Little is known of Hexham before about the early 760s, when Queen Etheldreda (or Ethelthryth) gave the site to Bishop Wilfrid of York to build a monastery. There is no archaeological evidence for anything earlier, but the name itself indicates a presence there in Anglo-Saxon times before Wilfrid. *Hagustaldes ea* is written in 681, and it appears that Hexham was land enclosed near to water by a younger

Hexham from the east.

son, a warrior who set out to find new land for himself. *Hagustalt* includes *hag*, an enclosure that also gave the hawthorn its name—a quickset hedge favoured for making an enclosure.

We have no idea of what the land looked like or was used for, but its position at a fording place on a bluff gives it a strategic value. To sustain a priory and church, lands were included in the gift, and money was certainly needed because the building was regarded by contemporaries as the finest this side of the Alps. Wilfrid, aristocratic, rich and well-travelled, brought to the building of the church his experience of architecture and rituals abroad. Convenient quarries of dressed stone were available on abandoned Roman sites—'the work of giants, crumbling', as one Anglo-Saxon poem describes them, ready to be recycled in this impressive building, of which little remains. The crypt is the most complete testimony to the importance of the building; here the pilgrims descended stone stairs into a narrow corridor that turned past an arched room where the relics of saints were displayed, then up again to the surface. If the pilgrims had time to look as they shuffled in the narrow corridors to get nearer the sacred centre, they might have seen geometrical patterns and lettering and tool marks on reused Roman stone, although much of it may have been covered with plaster. The dim light came from oil lamps or candles in niches. It was, and still is, a strange and moving place, and is only one of two such crypts in England, the other being at Ripon. Even without belief in the power of relics, its mystery and impact remain.

Hexham Anglian Crypt.

Vikings sacked it, rebuilding took place in Norman times; much of its present appearance is owed to the Augustinians. It lay in the conflict zone between England and Scotland, which resulted in the devastation of the nave. The rebuilding of the nave, indicated by some fifteenth-century masonry, was abandoned until 1907; it became a graveyard. When the tower and west walls needed attention, the digging for the foundation of a great buttress revealed the crypt, and it too became part of the cemetery. What we see today of the priory belongs mainly to the Augustinian period of rebuilding and the period 1850–1910. The attractive parkland that surrounds it away from the Market Place includes a fine bandstand, well-spaced trees, flowers and bushes. The Cowgarth Burn disappears under the bandstand and reappears beside a bowling green.

Essentially the Abbey is a place of worship, the town church. To some it is a museum. It attracts many visitors, and has to be staffed constantly by volunteers who act as guides and custodians. Its popularity creates problems, especially when some protest that they cannot look around when a service is taking place! It is very much alive by being used for music and drama. The arrival of a 30 foot (10 m) dragon on the parapet at the top of the Night Stair was a drama in itself. Its huge head moved from side to side, its jaws opened, and it breathed smoke and light.

On this occasion the Abbey absorbed a local legend that has many traditional ingredients of fairy stories. Known as 'The Spindlestone Dragon' the play took

1. Blawearie house.

2. Old Bewick Moor: the excavation site has now blended into the landscape.

3. Old Bewick Hill prehistoric marked rock.

4. Old Bewick church interior detail.

5. Piper's Hill from Branxton churchyard.

6. Ford Castle.

Above: **7.** Hexham abbey altar.

Left: **8.** Hexham Abbey sunlight through stained glass.

Opposite page:

Above: **9.** Blyth harbour.

Below: **10.** The treehouse in Alnwick Castle Gardens.

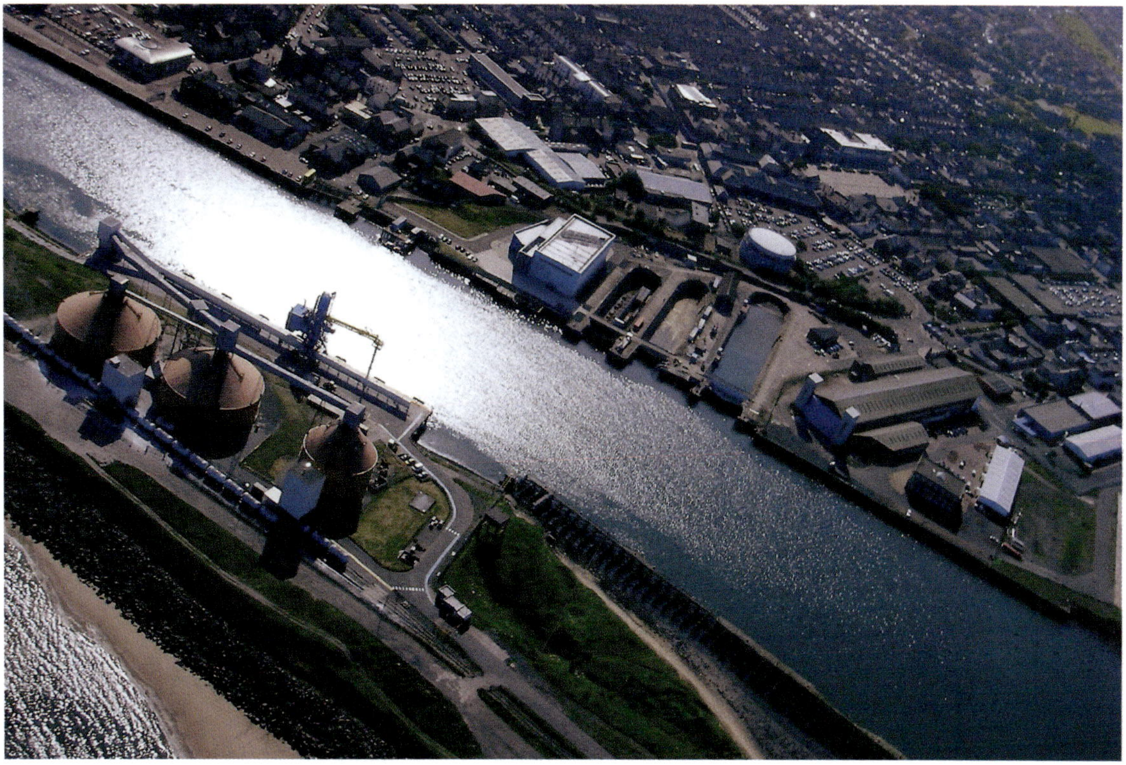

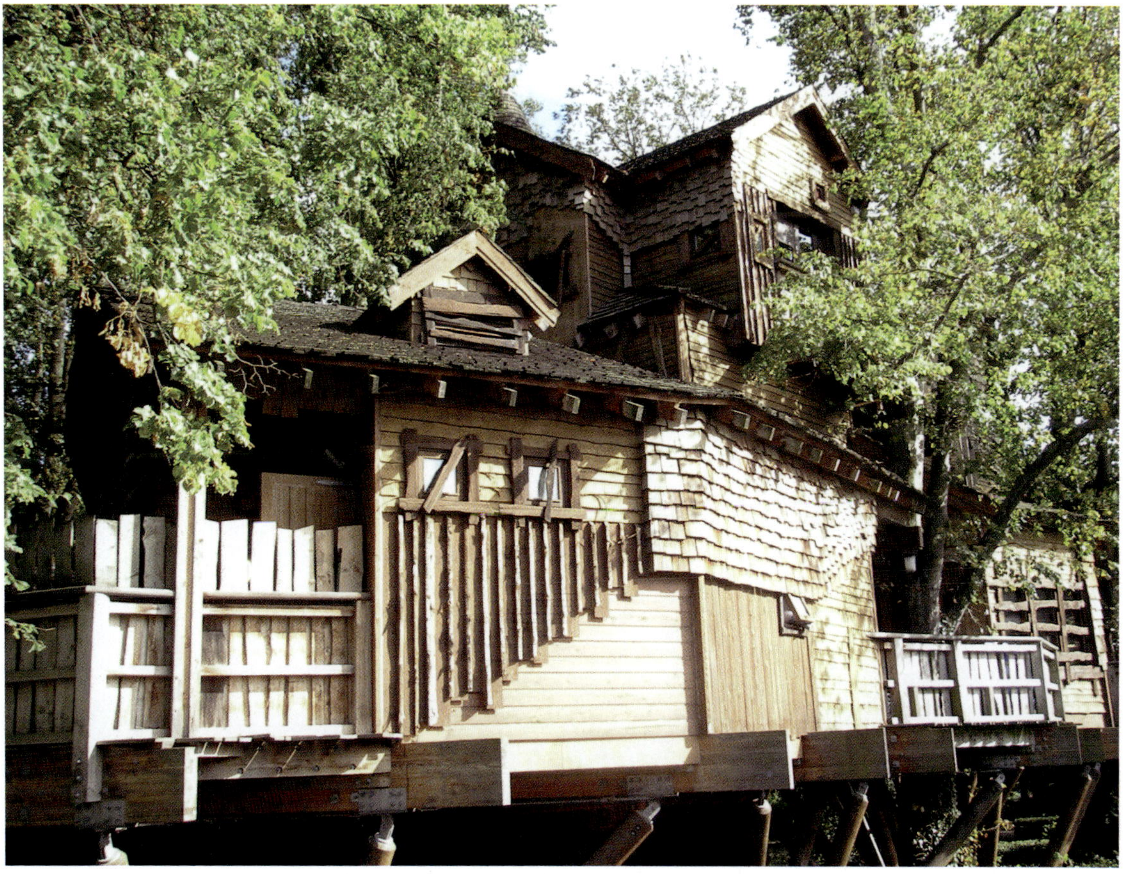

11. Helen Clark's mural of the treehouse—in Alnwick bus station.

12. Alnwick's Hotspur Gate which breaches the town wall.

13. Belsay Castle.

14. Amble harbour.

15. Halton towerhouse with an added wing.

16. Kirknewton church in the Glen Valley of the Cheviot Hills.

17. Dunstanburgh Castle.

18. Chilingham wild white cattle.

Left: **19**. Coastal rock-formation at Howick.

Below: **20**. Gordon Highmoor's impression of prehistoric cairn rocks.

Opposite page:

Above: **21**. Holy Island north: Norman architecture.

Below: **22**. The Ingram Valley, looking east.

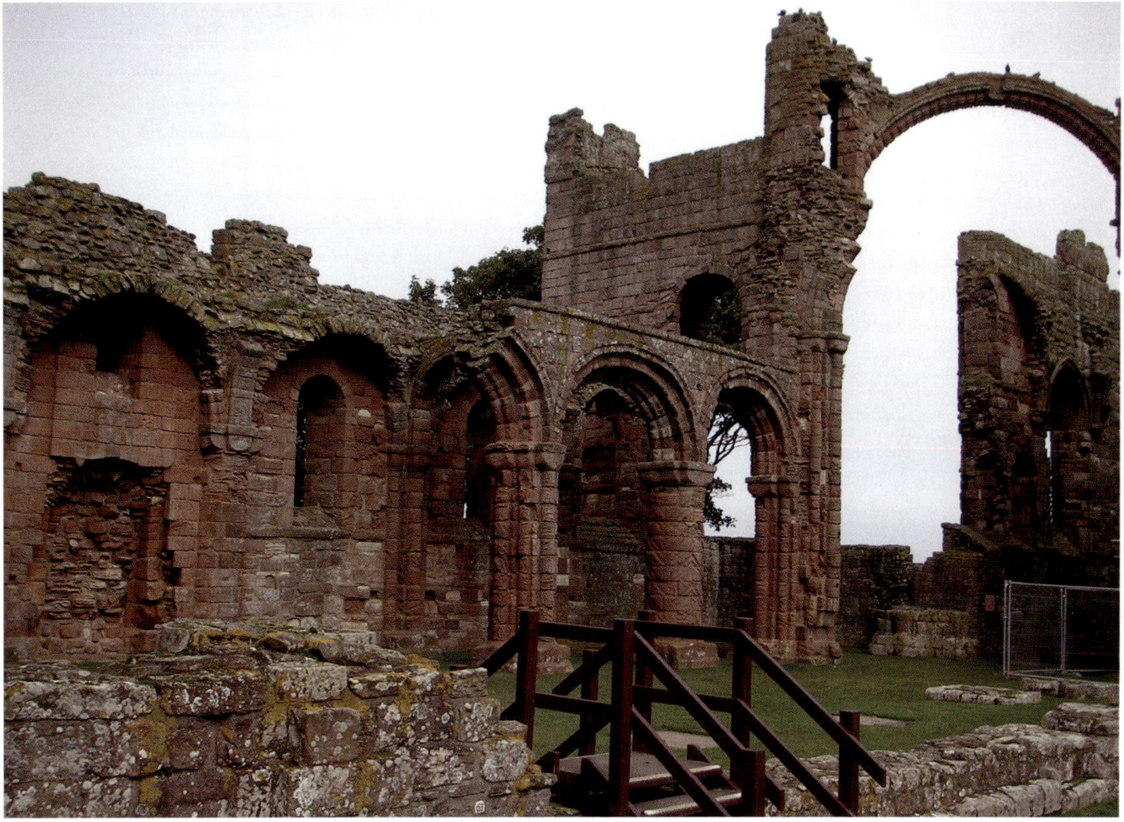

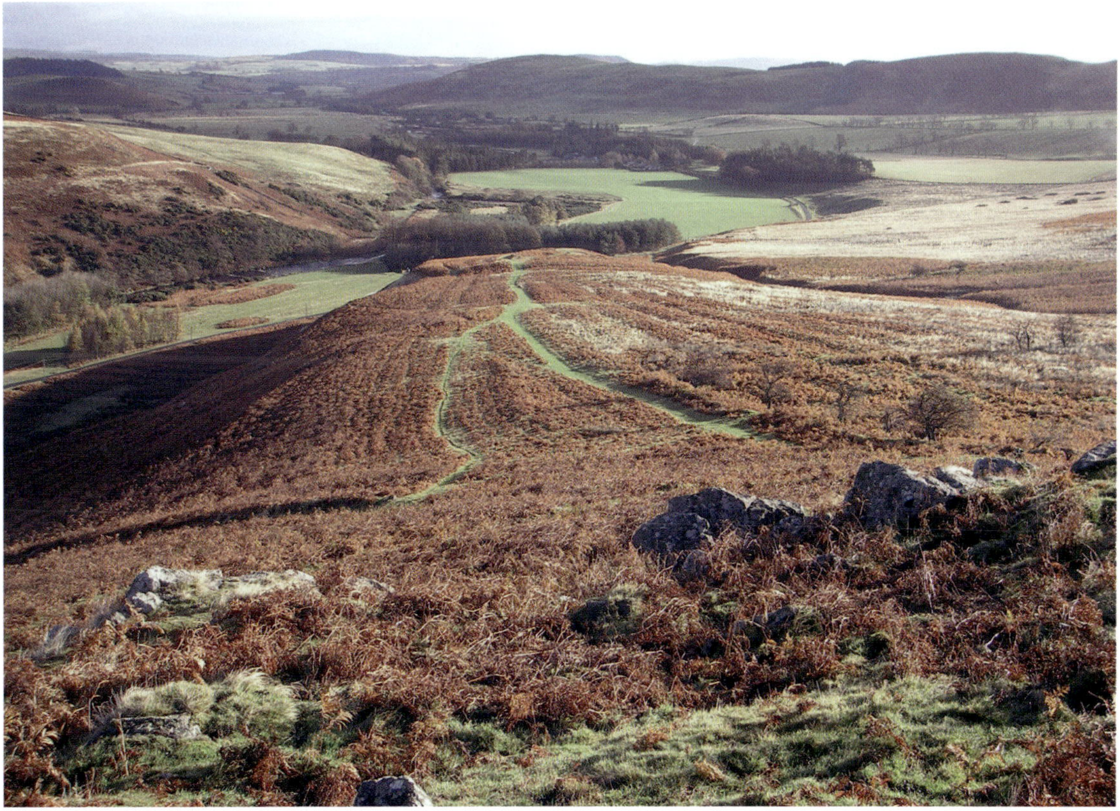

23. Cultivation terraces and rig and furrow in the Ingram Valley.

24. The Roman Wall, looking east.

25. Part of The Tyneside Archaeological Society survey team with the shepherd at Ravensheugh.

26. From the Vindolanda bathhouse over the main fort during excavations.

Above: **27.** Edlingham, with viaduct and castle at the bottom of the valley.

Left: **28.** Helen Clark's selection of Northumberland images.

Opposite page:

Above: **29.** A Hexham pear tree, cloister garth and east wall.

Below: **30.** Roughting Linn.

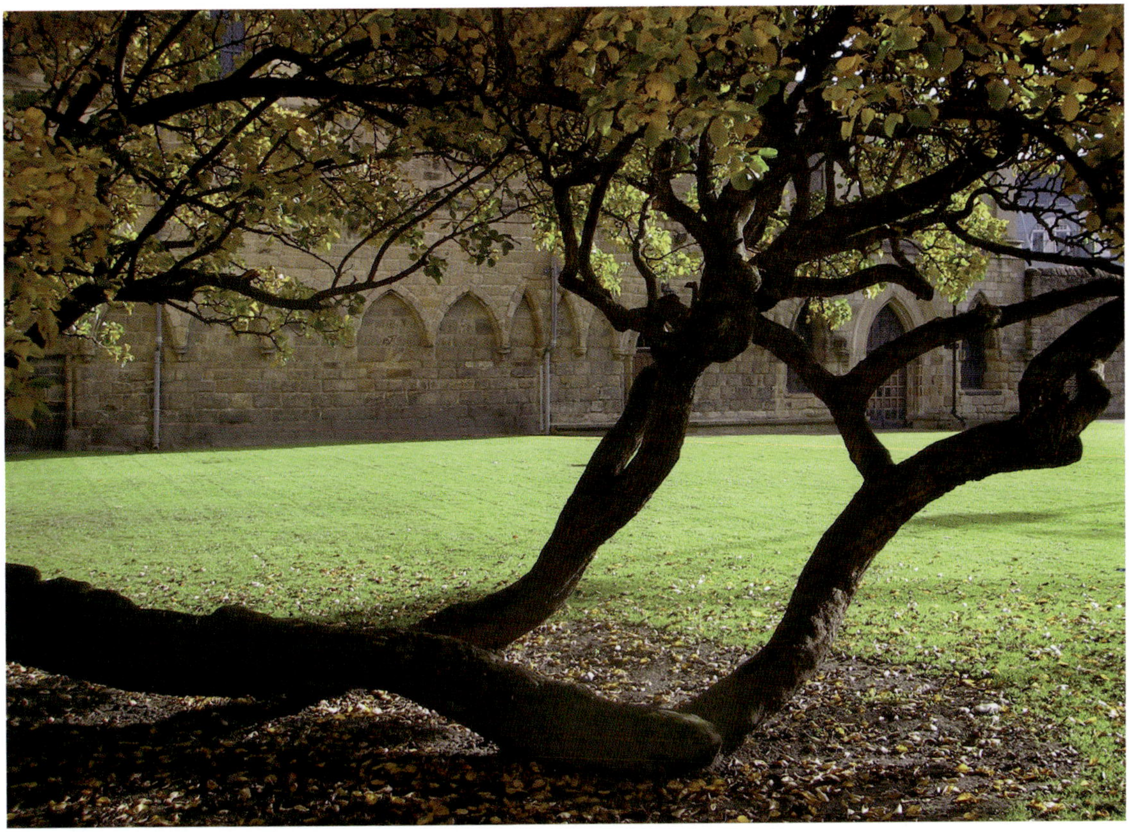

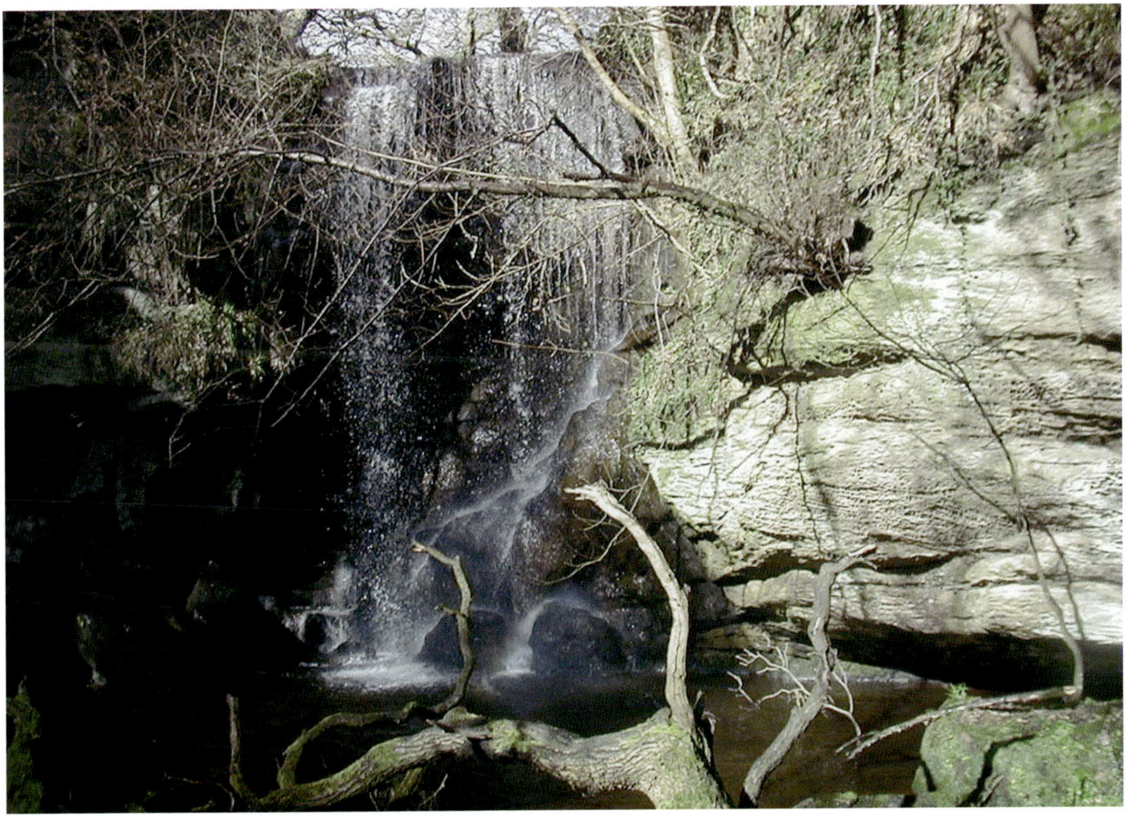

31. Hexham Abbey: a major project, where the new entrance on the line of the cloister leads to 'The Big Story'.

its story from the place near Bamburgh where a widowed king unwisely married a witch. She overheard her stepdaughter's beauty being praised above her own (shades of 'Snow White') and turned the Princess into a dragon in a fit of jealousy. The dragon was sustained by local people with troughs of milk. The young Prince, sensing that something was wrong, returned from abroad, taking the precaution of fitting his ship with a mast of birch and white sails to counter the forces of evil. The queen and her followers wrecked his ship, but he swam to safety, located the dragon in its cave, and tried in vain to kill it. When it warned him, 'Unless you kiss me three times, you will never see your sister again', he did so. There stood his sister, and the tale of evil was told. The Prince, with his own special powers, turned the witch into a toad, where it remains at Bamburgh.

Stories like this have enormous potential for improvised drama. The struggle between good and evil, of darkness against light are at the core. So is the presence of malice and hatred. Yet good triumphs. Young people with whom I have improvised these themes have delighted in creating the power and malice of witches and warlocks. They have also explored and approved the simple lives of ordinary Bamburgh folk, their jokes and games, their growing resistance to evil and the shock of subjugation to tyranny. To relieve the tension and bad atmosphere of the Dark Forest and the power of evil, one group invented a character called Liverfluke;

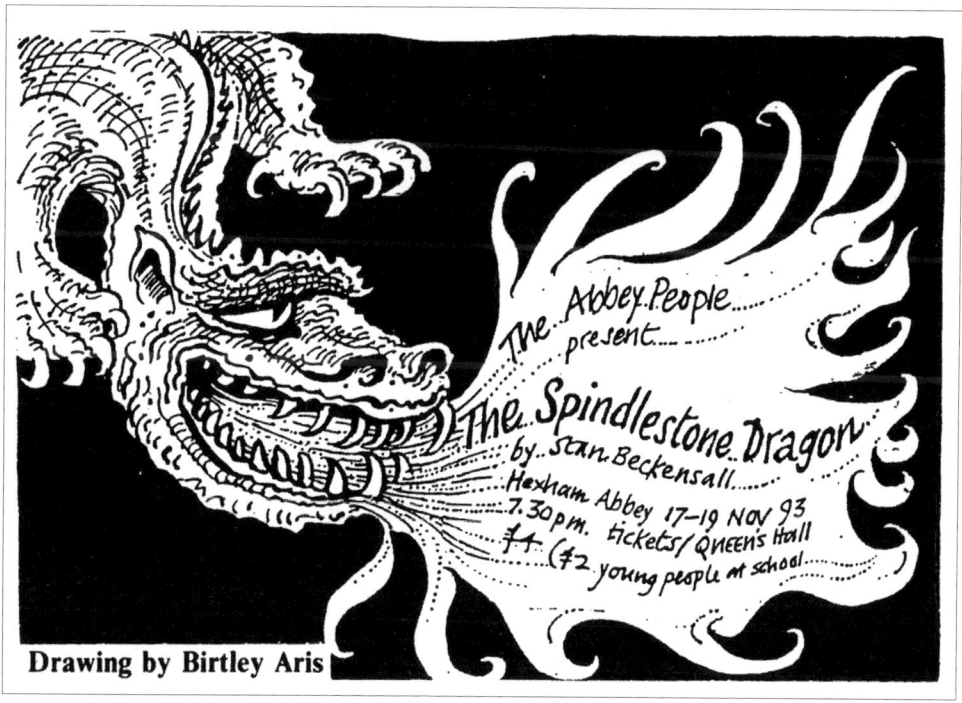

The Spindlestone Dragon play poster for an Abbey performance.

a warlock who liked all the 'wrong' things such as light and goodness. He was instrumental in the defeat of the queen. Perhaps, though, the scene that stood out among the rapid narrative action was when a family of beachcombers (mum, dad, two children) found the Prince's sword after the supernaturally raised storm, cleaned it, and legally kept it. The Prince tracked them to their home, persuaded them to return his sword and to lead him to the dragon's lair. The little girl insisted that the dragon was beautiful and not malignant, but the Prince had to find out for himself. This led to a futile fight and to the restoration of the Princess to normality. At once the darkness over the land began to lift, people sensed the change in the air, and were freed into action against their evil oppressors. When drama is used in this way the processes of exploration, of improvisation and role-play are all-important. If they result in something worth polishing and performing for others, so be it. The Abbey and all that it stands for, all that it has silently witnessed, is an appropriate place to act it out.

On another occasion people have listened to Thomas Becket, dressed in robes that had been made after consulting experts at Canterbury Cathedral, as he preached from the Abbey pulpit to an audience surrounded by the whole cast, carrying lighted candles. He foretold his martyrdom; having been through the temptations to use power for himself and for the Church, sustained by his own pride, he at last realised that he must do the right deed for the right reason by completely surrendering to the will of God. He must wish for nothing for himself, not even the glory of martyrdom. A full Abbey choir sang in the south transept throughout the play to heighten so many great moments in T. S. Eliot's great drama. His death took place at the top of the Night Stair.

For the last play performed in the 1990s, the north transept became the stage. In *Shepherds, Rogues and Angels* young and old, actors and musicians, enacted the story of Chaucer's *The Pardoner's Tale*, *The Second Shepherds' Play* from the Wakefield Cycle and *Everyman*. The climax of the plays was delivered by the Visitor, someone who had come to assess the spiritual health of the people and to advise them. For a conclusion I chose to use the writing of Alcuin of York (735–804) as the basis for a speech that included this:

> Beneath these floors, the bones of saints
> Are relics of a past that gives us strength.
> They urge you now: bring honour to your church,
> Clear be your task and careful be your word.
> Be yours an open hand, a merry heart,
> Christ in your mouth, LIFE, that all may know
> It's Christ you serve.
> Let none come here and sadly go away.
> Bring hope to all the poor, and solace to the sad,
> So they who follow you will reach the stars.
> Sow living seeds, words that are quick with life,
> That faith may be the harvest in men's hearts.

In word and in example let your light
Shine through the darkness like the morning star,
And let not riches flatter you and silence truth.
Nor king, nor canon, judge, nor yet your dearest friend
Muzzle your lips from righteousness.

Reference to the dead who lie under the flagstones was pertinent at the time, for we had reburied those that had been disinterred during the laying of paving stones to the south outside the chancel. This disturbance had begun in 1990 when trenches were dug across the Market Place to house BT cables. The narrow trenches, up to 3 feet (1 m) deep gave us a chance to see that the Market Place had always been an open space. It was when the cutting of the trenches moved across Beaumont Street to the Abbey that I literally came face to face with the dead.

Viewers of *Time Team* and *Meet the Ancestors* are familiar with some archaeological techniques, and appreciate that nothing is straightforward. It was well known that Beaumont Street had cut through the canon's graveyard, and there were sufficient marked slabs dug up in the past and displayed in and around the Abbey to establish who they were. The trenching of a public road was not considered to need a 'watching brief', but we did watch voluntarily and prevented the removal of bones that might otherwise have gone to a landfill site. A thin trench, about 3 feet (1 m) deep with a horizontal pipe running through it, provided a cross-section of this cemetery. At the base, undisturbed but polluted by petrol and diesel from the road, were skeletons that lay on their sides, faces to the south and arms at their sides, so closely packed that one overlay another. Above that was a more disturbed mixture of soil, a lens of lime, a piece of Roman stone, part of a red sandstone slab and a jumble of bones that lay just below the pavement.

Our objectives, made possible by a pause in the work, were to keep as many of the bodies as possible intact and to seal them in. Those already disturbed by the mechanical digger and by our cleaning up the section were to be taken away for specialist examination, and then returned to the Abbey for reburial. Dr Iain McCleod, living locally, was a dental pathologist with strong interests in archaeology that he has continued to pursue in Scotland. Dr Bill Cunningham, a local GP, recorded all the bones in situ.

The two skeletons at the bottom of the trench, lying on their right sides, may have been pre-Conquest. One was an old man, his head lying under a young man's legs. There was no sign of coffin or shroud, and the men appeared to have been packed into a limited space. Above them was great disturbance, but in all there were the fragmentary remains of about 16 individuals. The substantial parts of five showed they were men between 20 to 60+. They were well built and had led relatively healthy lives. Their teeth were worn in such a way that they must have eaten a coarse diet; as there was little dental decay they must have had a diet low in fermentable carbohydrate.

An excavation in 1993 when 'floorscaping' began revealed rows of bodies lying on their backs, and the site of a fourteenth-century chapel or sacristy. Only the

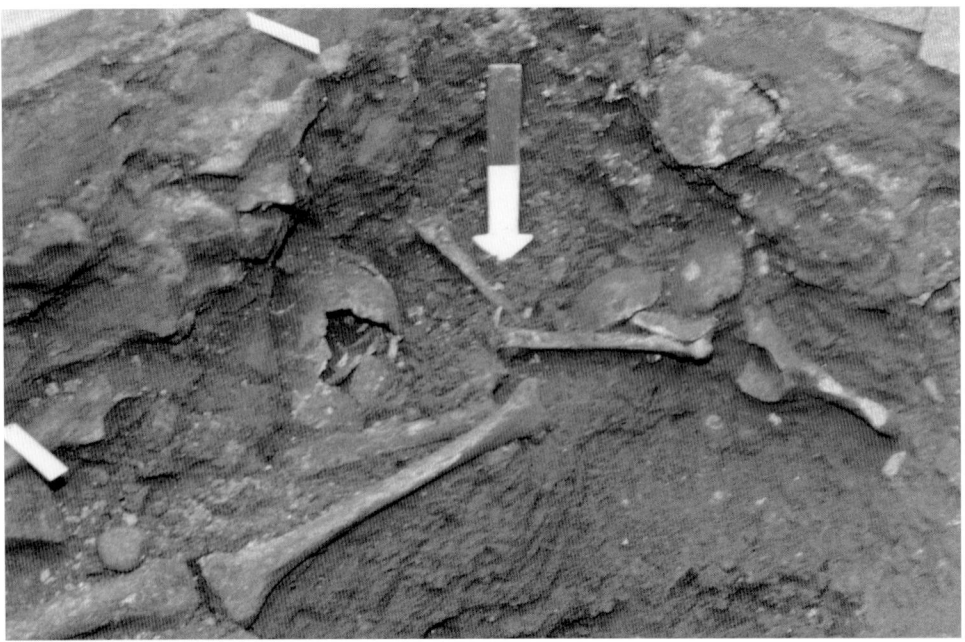

Skeletons to a depth of 1 m disturbed by Public Works in 1990 on the site of Hexham's canonical cemetery.

A woman's burial by the east chancel external wall. (*Peter Ryder*)

bodies at the top were removed; it was clear that many more were packed below. Some had fragments of named grave slabs near them. The east end of the Abbey was also investigated, where two large charnel pits, used during the late nineteenth century during the rebuilding of the east end of the church, were found.

There was an unusual burial of a woman in a stone-lined cist type of grave beside the south wall of the choir. She was around 5 feet 3 inches (1.60 m) tall, aged over 50, and had massive layers of calculus on her teeth. She suffered severely from arthritis, two of her neck bones being fused, and she had acute arthritis in her right foot. She had mild osteoarthritis of the right hip, and would therefore have had great pain from her back and neck, right foot and hip long before her death. Who she was and why she was buried there is not known. She and others excavated had been buried in sacred ground. What should archaeologists do with such remains? We solved the problem by 'keeping them at home'. Those disturbed by deep trenching in 1990, but still in position, were given a ceremony of reburial by the curate on the spot, with the workmen and others present. Sand was poured onto a grid of metal, and the remains sealed in concrete. The parts that had been removed were reburied in the north transept after a single floor slab had been removed and the space below excavated. A service for their reinterment was held after Evensong, and the choir sang a 'Nunc Dimittis'.

The same happened to the larger group of skeletons, and this time I was lucky to find a new grave for them under the slabs of the transept where the old heating ducts had been. Excavation of this area revealed a mixed soil, some pieces of coal and pottery, which filled the space down to a floor of mixed brick and stone; the sides were similarly lined. The service for them was attended again by worshipers after Evensong, the choir sang and this time it was attended by a Sikh doctor from UNESCO who had taken small DNA samples. He and his family, with representatives of organisations involved in the excavations, made this a memorable occasion.

Christian beliefs hold that the spirit is eternal and the body temporary. Bones, once they have given up their information, should not however be swept aside. Each generation must respect the care that is taken over the burial of the dead, and it was for me a time of satisfaction and relief and deep emotion when these now-familiar people found their new resting place. We do not know their names, but some of the slabs found during other disturbances may belong to them. Canon Walter, Robert of Kirkbride, Henry of Walton, John of Dalton and Robert of Bedlington are just a few of the names we know. This brings us closer to people.

It is impossible to describe all the features of this Abbey, but this poem that I wrote after a Candlelight Concert, a main event each year in the Hexham Abbey Festival, sums it up:

Hexham Abbey: Candlelight

Enter. You meet prayer-soaked stone
Invested with soft light, broken by stained glass.
You meet wood, warmed with time,
Darkened by caring, polished by use.
You meet images in paint:
Hollow-eyed Death, presiding over
The dance of the feckless and unsuspecting.
Here are lines of bishops and saints
Stretching in strips, with snatches of story.

Time spins and spirals all in one blend.
Brittle fragments of the Empire that was Rome,
Bundled Gothic pillars, black-edged in strong sunshine shafts,
An order of mind transformed to order by hands
That wield chisel and mallet.
Arches glimpsed through arches,
Soaring out of sight, upwards,
Light lingering on light.
Shadows shifting, corners hiding.

Listen now.
Bass from deep-throated organ pipes
Rends the foundations on which arches lie.
Light notes float among the curves
And thread among patterned stones.
Add candlelight: the melting shapes
Make tableaux of their own,
White stalactites, winged angels,
Birth and crucifixion all in one.
The soft, light touch of candle flame
Strokes the arch's throat, bends pillars inward.
Golden clerestory holds its shadows on a gentler rein,
And human faces are transformed
By wonder and an inner light.
All things conspire to lift the soul above the earth
From which this Abbey grows.
The tiny parts fail by themselves to move;
The way they blend
Disturbs us to the roots.

THE MARKET PLACE

The removal of some skeletons and the relaying of flagstones was a final step that brought the town right up to the walls of the Abbey. A painting of the 1820s and many black and white pen drawings of the Market Place remind us of how far that process has gone. Originally a wall, still visible in places, ran all round the Priory grounds, with an impressive round-arched gateway giving access from Market Street. It has now mostly been built over. A row of chapels attached to the east end of the Abbey abutted the wall, and these fell into decay. Secular buildings began to use the chapel fabric. Above them towered the east end with a rose window (also referred to as 'The Catherine Wheel') inserted in 1725, which fell out and brought down much of the wall with it. Plans for restoring the east end included the destruction of the east chapels once the buildings that clung to them were removed and showed how much money would have been needed for their restoration. Dobson in 1858 agreed that they should be demolished, and his plan to replace the whole east end with a design based on Whitby Abbey was put into operation.

The extent of the buildings to the south of the chancel survives in pictures and plans. They too were swept away, and in 1861 Beaumont Street was cut through the Priory precinct. Skeletons were then reported 'peering from almost every square foot of earth' and no one bothered to record or rebury them. The

Hexham Abbey east.

scheme swept away houses, a bakery, pigsties, privies and a sawmill. It made it possible for townsfolk to use the 'Slype' entrance to the Abbey that linked cloisters to chapter house and cemetery without running a gauntlet in the 'Long Backside'.

The basic arrangement of Market Place surrounded by buildings remains, although their structures and uses have changed. A view from the air shows a town clustered around Priory, Moot and Gaol, streets leading into it having strips of land for houses, yards and small workshops. To the south facing The Shambles a row of buildings hides the remains of a rectangular medieval church, once used by the townspeople. When the fish and chip shop recently caught fire, a survey before rebuilding (declared 'A Plaice in History' by Peter Ryder) demonstrated once again the extent and nature of this church building, with the remains of pillar bases in cellars. Hexham has many cellars, as the centre was so built up that they provided additional accommodation. This has led to stories about underground passages leading to the Priory; for what purpose we are not told. The decay of the town church made it impossible to use for services, which saved the priory church from destruction. We can now look at the event when Lionel Gray and Robert Collingwood came to 'dissolve' the Priory.

They did see many persons assembled with bills, halberds and other defenceable weapons like men ready to defend a town in time of war. And in their passing the common bell of the town was rungen, and straight after the sound of it, the great bell of the monastery was likewise rung, whereby the people forcibly assembled towards the monastery, where the said Lionel and Robert found the gates and doors fast shut. And a canon, called the Master of Ovingham, uttered these words: 'We be 20 brethren of this house, and we shall die ere that ye shall have this house.' The said Lionel and Robert said, 'Advise you well and speak with your brethren, and then give us answer finally.' And so the master departed into the house, and after his departure did come five or six the canons with divers other persons, like men of war in harness with swords girt about them, having bows and arrows and other weapons, and stood upon the tower and leads in the defence of their house, the said Lionel and Robert being without. About them did come and congregate many people, both men with weapons and many women. And so the said Lionel and Robert returned to meet the rest of the commissioners, and all together recoiled back to Corbridge, where they lay that night.

This was only a delay; in 1537 a royal army arrived, the Priory was dissolved and the canons were pensioned off or transferred to other duties. Carnaby, whose arms appear on a building to the west of the abbey, was given the local lands and properties.

A gentler era followed the accession of James I, although there were many cases of violence reported to the Manor Court. In 1761 a horrendous event marred the general peacefulness of the area. It is known as the Hexham Riot.

THE HEXHAM RIOT

Local people were called to the Moot Hall where conscripts to the Militia were to be selected. This was a kind of selective National Service. Trouble was anticipated; troops were drafted to the Market Place 'in order to put a stop to riotous assemblies'. The local people refused to be balloted for military service. William Allen, an officer of the North Yorkshire Militia, described what happened as the situation became tense. He reported people packing into the town and insulting his troops.

He said of his men that 'they bore it with greatest coolness and moderation. At one o'clock, or a little after, the proclamation was read, and they were acquainted with the penalty if they did not disperse. They still continued to wave their monstrous sticks, clubs and quarter staffs in the most insolent manner, over the heads of our men, for by this time they had come within reach of our bayonets, with which our front rank charged, and soon after they made a vigorous effort upon our left and broke in upon them'. Shooting broke out, 'upon which the word of command was given to fire, as it became an act of necessity and self-defence'.

He described the aftermath of the slaughter: 'And now we had an opportunity of contemplating the bloody scene before us, 24 being left on the spot, 18 of whom were dead and the rest dangerously wounded'. The next day was wet 'which was of service, as it washed the remains of yesterday out of the Market Place'. 52 civilians were killed and 44 wounded. A warrant was issued for the arrest of 17 others in connection with the riot.

When Peter Patterson of Shilvington was tried for High Treason and found guilty, they wrote of him as 'one of 500 persons and upwards armed and arrayed in a warlike manner' who 'waged and levied public war against our lord the King'. He was 73. He was drawn upon a hurdle to the place of execution in Morpeth. He stated that he did not think the crime he suffered was worthy of death. He survived falling off the cart with the rope around his neck when the rope broke. A new rope was found, while he waited. He was hanged again, cut down, drawn and quartered.

The longest survivors of the Riot were Samuel Carter and Cornelius Ridley. Samuel was lamed for life, and his mother, Sarah, pregnant at the time, was killed in the Riot. He made spinning wheels, and died in 1825. Cornelius Ridley, 12 at the time of the Riot, was shot through the mouth and became a cordwainer, dying in 1828. Both men were respected Hexham citizens and leading figures in the independent church.

The reader is left to evaluate this serious address preached in the Abbey Church to the common people:

> O foolish People and unwise!
> How unmindful are you of the rich Blessings of Providence? How ungrateful to the best of kings and the mildest administration? How little have YOU felt the miseries of war? Alas! I fear your very Prosperity makes you wanton; your very Liberty tempts you to be licentious. You are apparently discontented with your low situation in life, and therefore begin to hate and envy all in authority. Do but turn impartial eyes back upon your late Behaviour: how inconsistent was it with the amiable character of BRITONS?

How contrary to every appearance of loyal subjects? And how unworthy the Behaviour of reasonable Men; but much more of sober CHRISTIANS?

What infatuation could move you to such daring, such Treasonable Attempts?

Many of you vainly imagine, perhaps, that you mean no harm; nor did you go with any bad or bloody designs. But did your presence give countenance to this MAD and WICKED action?

The Militia Law, you say, is a very bad one, and therefore ought to be repealed. How? Are YOU the only proper and infallible judges of what is or is not expedient for the Good and Well-being of the whole community? How came men of your rank by this extraordinary knowledge? Matters of state are much above you.

Repent of your Folly. Let this be a severe warning to you. Meddle not hereafter with things above your capacity. Be Humble and Content. And if our gracious sovereign shall think fit, out of mere mercy and tenderness, to make but A FEW EXAMPLES among you, for such a daring, heinous crime, be you that escape ever duly thankful for the great and undeserved lenity shown towards you.

Antiquarian interest has focused on the medieval buildings that are most impressive and still visible, but there has been in Hexham a number of very competent historians who are looking, or have looked at other aspects. Until recently, for example, documents on seventeenth-century Hexham had remained unread, and the wealth

The site of some of Hexham's tanneries, a major town industry.

of information in local newspapers had been little used. In the seventeenth century leather was a major industry in Hexham, although it is unusual for a small town to be so specialised. In a market town, the slaughter of animals, the curing of skins, tanning, and the manufacture of items such as high quality gloves were a major source of employment, some of which could be carried out in people's homes.

Names such as 'Tanners' Row', 'The Skinners' Arms' (renamed 'The Old Tannery' and then turned back again), 'Glovers' Place' between the town centre and the Tyne indicate such industries, and the Public Swimming Pool has retained the imposing façade of a wool warehouse. The Local History Society, one of the largest in the north, has investigated and published a survey of part of this manufacturing area, Cockshaw, with all its changes in use, architecture and people. It is easy to forget that Hexham was once a very overcrowded and dirty place, with polluted burns, the smells of tanning pits and of human and animal refuse. The Borough Books, records of the manor court, which regulated such things as petty crime and public nuisance, have frequent accounts of attempts to keep the burns clean. In 1661 it was ordered that:

> No inhabitants in or about this town shall wash any puddings (animal intestines) in the west burn called the Abbey Garth Burn or in Cockshaw Burn, or shall wash any filthy things in either of the same burns until they come to George Leadbitter's house being the nethermost house in the town upon pain of *6s 8d*.

Despite the large fine, there were frequent prosecutions for 'pudding washing' and the washing of raw wool and skins. There were attempts to prevent tanners and glovers from emptying their 'lime pits, dubs and baits betwixt four o'clock in the morning and five in the afternoon.' Attempts were made to restrict people to cleaning out pits to the autumn months when there was more chance of the accumulated filth being washed into the river, but frequent prosecutions showed that these were not successful. We thus have in the seventeenth century an unpleasant picture of an area crossed by burns carrying a lethal cocktail of waste from the leather industry, human waste and other rubbish. Anna Rossiter's research has made possible a detailed account of this working area of Hexham in the seventeenth century.

The problems were to continue and intensify, and information from Census returns and Public Health reports reveal that parts of Hexham were grossly overcrowded and unhealthy. There is an area named Holy Island, formed by the two streams that flow past it; there were many non-established places of worship around it. In 1871 there were 27 families of 115 people housed in a very small space. Yet this 'island' also has two of Hexham's most distinguished seventeenth-century houses.

Population in Britain rose dramatically in the nineteenth century, as it did in Hexham. Nineteenth-century Census returns show that about a third of Hexham's population was born elsewhere, many from townships in Northumberland, Durham and Cumberland, and we can trace the movement of some families by the birth-places of their children. And what a variety of occupations is revealed: cadgers, linen-weavers, cowkeepers, appraisers, hawkers, wool carders, hatters, tinsmiths,

Holy Island House, Hexham.

whitesmiths, straw bonnet makers, mendicants, lead ore washers, chimney sweeps, a keeper of prison (unemployed), and washerwomen. These were in addition to market gardeners and to the leather industry occupations, and when the latter declined there are other occupations such as painters, florists, grocers, drapers, stone masons, butchers, mailcart drivers, dressmakers and domestic servants, to take their place. Towards the end of the nineteenth century more workers found jobs as traction engine drivers, grooms, postal employees, railwaymen and coachmen. There was a constant demand for workers in building and allied trades as old houses fell into decay and new developments emerged. People continued in work much later in life than they do today.

This is only a brief snapshot of what research into documents can reveal about the lives of people who seldom have any mention in histories. One further source fills in the picture a little more. Central government took action in Public Health, and the publication of Rawlinson's Public Health Report in 1853 was a strong condemnation of conditions in the town. The water supply came in for particular criticism, for the link between filthy water and bad sanitation and lethal diseases was realised, although there were people who wanted to gloss this over because putting it right would cost them money. His map locates privies, ashpits, slaughterhouses and water channels, and the text fills in the picture. Here are just a few examples of what he reported.

Streets were irregularly planned, houses of unequal height, and everything cramped and mixed up with 'pigsties, privies, cesspools and foul middens.' Streets were dusty

Hexham Market Place east, a late-Victorian photograph.

in summer and muddy in winter, and drainage was chaotic. Water for drinking was generally impure. Very few ashpits and privies were cleaned once or twice a year. Refuse was dumped into well-like back yards, into the streets and into such places as the overcrowded graveyard that was already a major health hazard. 'Gilligate', the continuation of Market Street towards the Tyne, was described as 'even more noxious than all the other parts, with its thickly- populated houses, no privies, no drainage, and stagnant pools. In one case the drainage was so bad that all the filth oozed through the house walls and wet the beds.'

No wonder that this area had 65 cases of smallpox in four months in the winter of 1851.

Rawlinson stated that 'There is no local government power capable of grappling with the evils that have accumulated with the growth of the place; and it is a lamentable fact that the attempt to obtain this power by the cheapest accessible means is opposed.'

The report helped to put the finger on some of the greatest health hazards, but the Slum Clearance reports some 70 years later show that many problems of poor health and housing remained.

To the many tourists who come to Hexham today, much of this will be hidden, for it is a pleasant and healthy town. It has expanded away from the traditional centre with good quality housing that reflects some prosperity. When you stand by the 1901 drinking fountain in the Market Place, you may read W. W. Gibson's poem on its north side that enthuses about the places from which the waters flow.

> Beneath the open sky my waters spring
> Beneath the clear sky welling fair and sweet,
> A draught of coolness for your thirst to bring,
> A sound of coolness in the busy street.

His lines would not have applied to Hexham in Rawlinson's time!

The year 2000 saw work going on to rearrange the layout of the old Priory precinct and to improve the children's playground at the bottom of what is called The Sele (or Seal), an open space centred on a green hill. This parkland, protected from other building developments, includes a flower-bordered Bowling Green; it is one of the most gracious aspects of a town that has so much going for it. The Victorian buildings, notably the Queen's Hall, that line Beaumont Street, may have destroyed part of the priory grounds but have enhanced that area as an attractive approach to the market place. Hexham has preserved much of its past but has moved with the times. It is largely Victorian at its centre, and even its Abbey was considerably re-arranged in that period. The centre makes it small enough to be a good meeting place for all its residents, a place to worship, to shop, go to the cinema, dine, play

Hexham railway station, one of the earliest in England. (*Birtley Aris*)

bowls, swim and take the children to the playground. It gives the new residential areas that have spread outwards and up the hillsides an attractive and significant focus.

The most recent and far-reaching development at the Abbey is to convert those buildings that were confiscated at the Dissolution and then turned into a residence for Abbey use, including all sorts of facilities including an area for the telling of the story of Hexham and its Priory, and rooms where school children can come for a day to learn more about this.

WEST ALONG THE VALLEY

The Tyne has the ninth largest river basin in Britain, and the place where the North and South Tyne meet to the west of Hexham is at Warden. The two rivers flow on either side of a sandstone massif that forms a triangle of land rising to 280 m at its highest part in the north. The name means a lookout hill, borne out by the siting of early earthworks upon it.

This area gives us an ideal time-span characteristic of much of the county. Small scatters of flint and chert chippings on the sunny south-facing slopes tell of nomadic peoples who probably lived on the coast, but who used the river valleys to access hunting and gathering areas of the interior in a period that lasted from the end of the Ice Age to the beginning of settled farming. They carried the raw material of their technology with them to make the arrows, blades and scrapers essential to their hunting, and knapped it on the spot.

On the same slopes is a long mound that is possibly a Neolithic burial cairn made of cobbles collected from the surrounding area, not at the highest point, but where it could be seen from below and from which the river valley is overlooked. This could be about 5,000 years old. On the top of the hill are earthworks of roughly concentric rings and ditches, comparable to many similar structures known generally as pre-Roman 'hill forts'. This one has something special about it; when I photographed it from the air one February, the low sunlight threw into relief a complexity of other earthworks that had gone unheeded or unreported. These rectilinear enclosures and field walls cannot all be explained without excavation, but they do show that the site continued to be used for centuries, perhaps beginning with a Roman presence as the hill overlooks the first Roman boundary of the Stanegate, established before the Wall and its forts. The most likely use of some of the eastern enclosures is as animal pens.

To the east of these enclosures the land falls away to the north Tyne valley, on the slopes of which are well-defined terraces that were used for farming, possibly in prehistoric times and in medieval times. Quern stones for grinding corn have been found in the fort, so farming would have been both arable and pastoral.

Another layer of time is revealed by a Norman-type motte built on a ridge behind the vicarage. Although no excavation has taken place, it is possible to see it as one of the early defensive sites of the Norman Conquest, overlooking a small settlement to the east. Here the Saxon church tower built partly of stone recycled from Roman buildings echoes other such towers at Corbridge, Bywell and Ovingham.

Warden enclosures from the east.

A view of Warden Hill taken in strong winter sunshine, looking north-west.

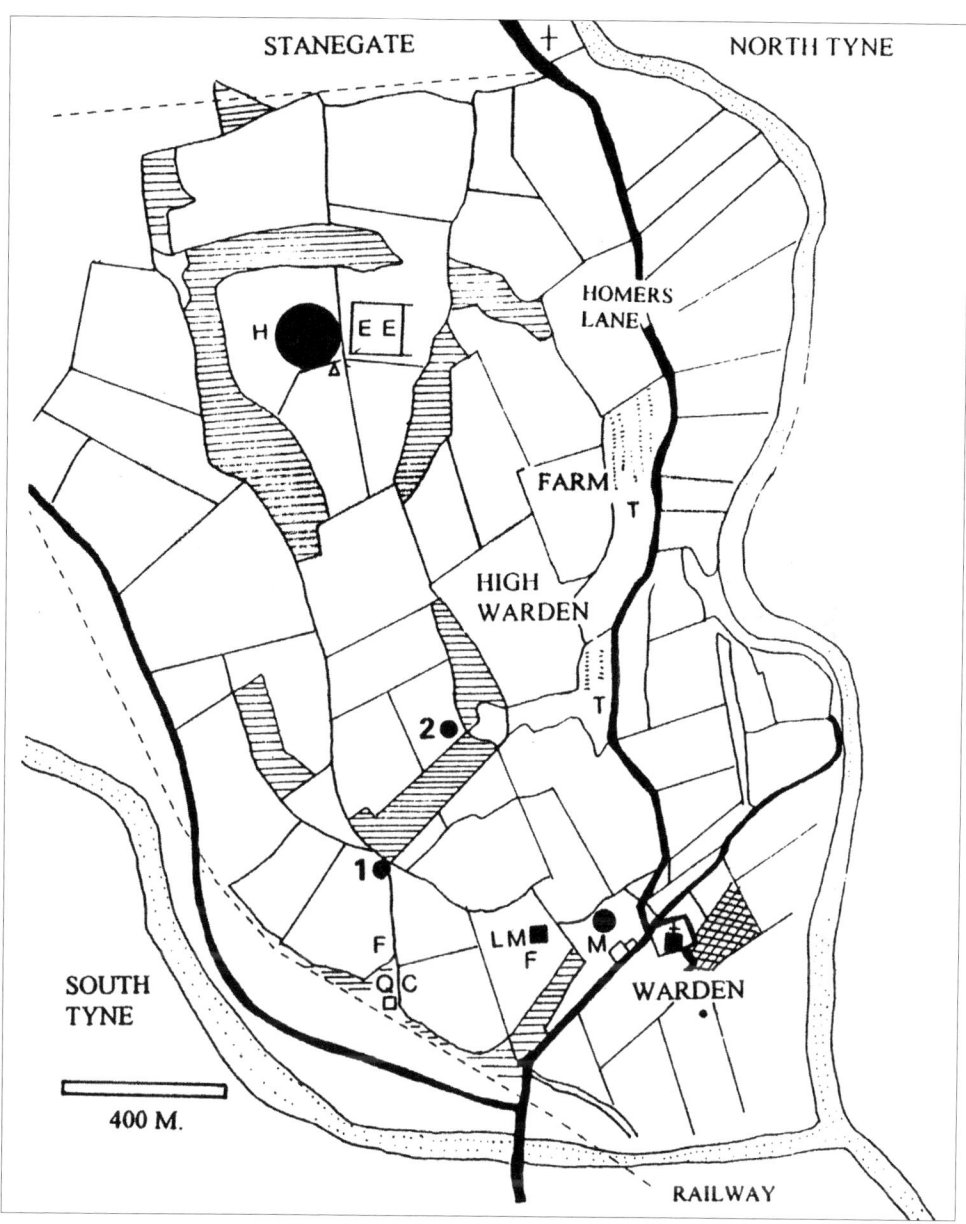

Warden: a sketch map to show many features from different periods.

KEY	
H	Hillfort
EE	Enclosures
T	Terrace
1 and 2	Mesolithic flint scatters
LM	Long mound
M	Motte

This very interesting hill is accessible by public footpaths that enable the walker to see all these features. The views from the top of the hill are splendid, taking in the Tyne valley to Hexham, the village of Wall and Chesters, Fourstones village and the whinstone ridges on which the Hadrian's Wall snakes westward.

West of Hexham, *Haydon Bridge* was a medieval village, half a mile to the north of the present small town that lies on either side of the River Tyne. The western part of the fourteenth-century chapel was demolished and the stone used in the building of the church of St Cuthbert in 1786 by the Greenwich Hospital Commissioners, who administered the confiscated estates of the Earl of Derwentwater, executed for his part in the 1715 Jacobite Rising. What is left of the old church was restored in 1882 by John Hodges. The earliest part of the church appears to be twelfth century, with the chapel being built two centuries later.

There is abandoned industry in the area, notably the remains of a lead mine, with its buddles (washing tanks) and other buildings visible. There was a Langley Barony Coal and Fireclay Company, Sanitary Ware manufacturers, which provided white crosses for the village cemetery in one of its uses.

At *Haltwhistle*, the recent building of a bypass has made a considerable difference to people's lives, as the main road was notoriously narrow there. The railway station on the Newcastle–Carlisle railway is very attractively restored and refurbished. The older part of the town has a splendid church, Holy Cross, lying south of the Market place with a view across the Tyne valley. Everywhere are signs of an industrial past. Whinstone was quarried, and a tubway led to the main railway line. There were limestone quarries, kilns, brickworks, two woollen mills, collieries, fireclay works and the Haltwhistle Gas Light Company (1856). The Ironworks was, like many others in the county, short-lived, from 1856–60s.

Before leaving this part of the county, a word about two brothers who have made their names known for quite different reasons. A notable son of Haydon Bridge was the painter John Martin, some of whose dramatic biblical paintings, such as Belshazzar's Feast and the Fall of Babylon are frequently on show in the Laing Art Gallery, Newcastle. His brother Jonathan is, sadly, remembered not for creation but for the destruction of part of York Minster. He served his time in Hexham as a tanner, went to London and was pressed into the navy. His mental derangement was revealed in the attacks he made on clergy; he would turn up at church and launch an attack on the whited sepulchres, and had to be physically restrained. His wrath found its full expression when he hid after a service in York Minster, waited until everyone had gone and locked up, and set fire to anything he could get his hands on. He escaped by ropes he had cut from the bells and made his way towards Hexham, where he was arrested at Codlaw Hill, near Wall. He had caused £60,000 worth of damage. His defence of his action was that he was doing God's will, and he made a full confession. He was jailed for the rest of his life in St Luke's Hospital, London, where he died nine years later in 1838. John, the painter, died in 1854, and his second brother, William, in 1851.

6

Some Townscapes, Small Settlements and Famous Spots

Hexham owes much of its position as a town to the establishment of a Saxon and, later, medieval priory. In the thirteenth century there was a stimulus that other towns shared of becoming a market and place where fairs were held; by the sixteenth century Hexham shared this status with Alnwick, Berwick, Bellingham, Haltwhistle, Morpeth and Wooler.

The Anglian settlements of Bamburgh, Warkworth, Corbridge and Rothbury became administrative centres, for they were royal estates. In the Norman period some small towns benefited by being protected by baronial castles; Alnwick and Warkworth were established as such.

WARKWORTH

We see how a moated castle with a ditch cut across the promontory formed by a U-shaped bend in the River Coquet guards access from the open south. The river is spanned by a lovely medieval bridge with a defended tollhouse. Between castle and church the main street is flanked by houses that have long thin strips of land running towards the river on both sides. These 'burgage' strips, or 'scribes', as they are known in Warkworth, are characteristic of medieval town plans, but they are seldom so clearly seen. The old town has an impressive approach from the bridge, with the land rising to the castle mound, in spring covered with daffodils. To the west of the street, the long nave of a Norman church with its particularly impressive vaulted chancel has been developed and added to, its spire being an unusual feature in this county. On the modern lectern, a pelican is feeding her young with drops of her blood, an image also carved in wood at Hexham Abbey. In King Lear, the king refers to his daughters as 'pelican' because they are feeding off his substance, a misapprehension that the pelican was giving its blood rather than smearing waterproofing oil from its feathers. The image however is appropriate: Christ giving his blood for his people. By coincidence, in the 1970s, a single pelican that was promptly named 'Percy' after the Dukes of Northumberland, began to live on

Warkworth castle.

Warkworth castle, an aerial view looking south-west.

the riverside, and was often seen walking across the grass in front of the castle. When he died he was stuffed and displayed in The Hancock Museum, Newcastle, a display that I cannot look at.

A Flower Festival and an innovative drama group are two aspects of an active village life. Before Word War II a Pageant had been an important event, and it was revived in 1977. I was lucky to be involved in the scripting and production, which drew upon many talents. Against the splendid architecture of the castle keep, surely one of the finest buildings in Britain, events spanning a hundred years of history were given a continuity by three men, the common people who did all the work, building the castle, tilling the fields, fighting battles, and even providing entertainment for visiting nobility. Amid all the changes in politics, they were constant. At Otterburn they had fought and been defeated. Harry Hotspur said farewell to his wife to fight the future Henry IV and was killed. Richard II had prophesied these events from the wooden stairs leading to the castle entrance. The men and their friends enacted Chaucer's story of 'The Pardoner's Tale', becoming the three men in search of Death, for visiting nobility at a banquet. For me there was a particular moment of wonder when a local stonemason took upon himself the role of narrator, explaining to the audience what a castle was for and how it was built, while the children mimed it in the background with their toys on the site of the church foundations there.

It became the fashion to have a battle as part of the play, and the local RAF provided the pyrotechnics that accompanied it on the ground. After the sound and fury there was silence as smoke filtered away and Henry IV came to acclaim his victory, but the 'three' had the last word, for a head teacher and two farmers from real life were still there after all the others had gone.

Working together on such a project (Pageants are now held every three years) gives a village an added sense of identity and purpose; in a place such as Warkworth with its riverside walks and vistas, it adds power to the place, for it continues to live and move and have its being. This happens too when local churches are filled with flowers and festivals, when village sports and fetes are lovingly organised, teams supported, and cultural and leisure time activities are regarded as an essential part of life.

ALNWICK

Alnwick has pursued a policy of attracting visitors into its once-walled town, where the castle, so dramatic and large in its setting, is already a magnet to many, among them filmmakers and TV crews. Basically a medieval, ducal town, the lion rampant and spur constantly remind us that this is one of the great power bases of the north. The centre of the town is the meeting place of ancient roads, still apparent in its triangular centre. Names such as Fenkle Street (at an angle), Bondgate and Narrowgate remind us of roads coming through the town walls attached to the castle. The strips of land that have houses fronting the streets, despite later building, are still visible. Narrow streets suddenly open out at Bailiffgate, the area where troops

Alnwick Market Place.

could gather and where administration was housed. Here the main castle entrance is a fine barbican, a castle in its own right. The decorative stone human figures on top are relatively modern replacements of older ones, still seen on the keep. There is a wealth of interest in Alnwick that needs time to explore, not all of it ancient. For example, in 'The White Swan' there is a function room modelled on part of the 'Olympic', the sister ship of the 'Titanic'. The carved wooden panels, although obviously not Elizabethan, provided a good background to an Elizabethan Evening of words and music that Alnwick College once provided for the town during annual Fair Week. The college is closed; the fair goes on.

Cobbled streets, with a recently cleared and renovated Market Place attract international performance groups as well as markets, with furniture designed by local schools.

Among the interesting buildings, St Michael's is a rare example of a completely Perpendicular style church, surprisingly built at a time of Border wars in the fifteenth century outside the castle walls. Little is left of a Premonstratensian Abbey, but there is a well-preserved Friary in the Duke's Park, where the Brizlee Tower also rises spectacularly. For those who wish to look at more recent building developments, there is an interesting contribution of eighteenth- and nineteenth-century architecture. One of the finest buildings is the old railway station.

St Michael's church, Alnwick.

BERWICK-UPON-TWEED

Berwick was given a peculiar coat of arms depicting a bear and a wych elm tree, which shows a lack of understanding of how its name originated—as a farm or settlement that specialised in barley.

The town, despite its attractive appearance today, has suffered a horrifying history at the forefront of wars between England and Scotland and the constant disputes within the borders. Its strategic importance is emphasised by the Elizabethan defensive walls and bastions that provide a splendid walkway from which to view the town. Earlier fortifications were to the north, where the medieval castle is now breached by a railway, and where the Bell Tower still rises on the wall line. The town is full of interest. It has a rare parish church built during the Commonwealth period, Holy Trinity on Wallace Green, opposite the purpose-built barracks of 1717–21. It is a pleasure to explore buildings from the ramparts, such as the gunpowder store, with its buttressed walls and small rounded windows standing within a walled compound designed to take an accidental internal blast.

The town hall lies at its busy modern centre, crowded in the summer by holiday-makers from local caravan sites. It was built in 1754–61 south of Marygate, at the end of a road through the defences; a flight of steps leads to its porticoed entrance, impressive bell tower and spire.

The bridges that span the Tweed range from a red sandstone bridge of fifteen arches, 355 m (1,164 feet) long, completed in 1626, to the concrete road bridge and eventually to the great Royal Border Bridge of 1847–50 with 28 arches that carry the railway across. The river attracts flocks of birds, including many swans. A flourishing arts centre, The Maltings, is recent. Developments within the town have attracted some well-conducted archaeological excavations that are revealing more of its history.

Towns like Hexham, Alnwick and Morpeth lie on rivers inland, whereas Berwick and Warkworth are coastal. Much of Northumberland's industry lies on the coastal plain, with industries based on coal and other natural resources accounting for intensive building of brick houses, characteristic of so much of the coast. Power shifted from land to industrial wealth and commerce, although some of it was reinvested in the country. Despite the changes that heavy industry made, some towns managed to retain at least some signs of their earlier history, such as Newbiggin.

Some coastal industries have blended back into the landscape. Visitors to Holy Island generally spend most of their time at the Priory, Museum, parish church and castle, all of which are rich in interest, but there is an impressive group of lime kilns beyond the castle that marks the last of such ventures that began in 1344. Limestone was quarried, heated to about 1,000C and from two tonnes of limestone one tonne of quicklime was produced. When water was added it became slaked lime. The products were used for neutralising acids in soil, in mortar mixes and for whitewashing buildings, acting as a disinfectant. Single stone chambers in which wood was burnt were first used, but the gothic style of the arched block that we see on the coast houses six kilns, the flat tops of which are like circular chimneys. Inside are passages giving access for wagons and people to the draw holes that sucked air into the mixture of heated coal and limestone, and allowed the lime and slag to be taken out. Some of the slag is piled outside the kilns, now partially grassed over, the white lime and cinder still peeping through. The 'pots' could be constantly fed by coal; and lime emptied into them from the top from horse-drawn wagons.

One of the delights of Holy Island is a walk that follows the curve of the disused wagonway from the kilns, along the coast and into the dunes, to the Nessend quarries, and returns to the village by a 'green' road. Around the castle where it stands on the almost-vertical outcrop of whinstone are remains of the wagonway. One branch curves down to the coast, where some wooden pillars still mark the site of the jetty, now like some irregular wooden sea henge, to which ships bringing coal or taking away lime would tie up. One can picture the wagons being drawn up the slope to the pots and the lime and coal being emptied into chutes. There would have been considerable smoke, but the kilns lay away from the village.

The history of lime burning on Holy Island represents in some ways that of the rest of the county. Here it became uneconomical, and closed down in the 1860s. Lime kilns at Beadnell and Seahouses shared the same fate, but remain as attractive and interesting monuments. The variety and quality of design of similar structures all over the county is an added bonus for the explorer.

Berwick town. (*Newcastle University*)

Berwick 'Commonwealth' church.

Berwick bridges.

Holy Island Priory and castle.

Holy Island castle and wooden jetty from which lime was exported.

Holy Island Priory.

Above: Holy Island limekilns and the wagonway tracks to them.

Left: Holy Island Priory Norman arches.

Holy Island is a great spiritual centre, with an influence in Europe out of all proportion to its present size. As such, it receives thousands of visitors when the tides are right. The Causeway is paralleled by rows of poles that still mark an alternative crossing for walkers. The blossoming of faith and learning and the destruction of its material culture by Viking raids, the story of those who wandered around the north with Cuthbert's body before it reached its final resting place in Durham cathedral, are well documented. It is only recently that some attempts have been made to protect the harbour and other areas against chaotic car parking that almost obscured the harbour.

There is nothing to be seen of the early Christian monastery, and the Norman Priory built in red sandstone on its site is a ruin with eroded stone having a life and beauty all of its own. But the parish church of St Mary has features that suggest that it is older than its refounding in 1083, and it is one of the places on the island where visitors are not just invited to view a museum, but to witness the work of that church founded so many years ago continuing.

There is much more to be said and written about this island, but I offer a poem that began with the name Lindisfarne. In 730 it was *insula Lindisfarnensis*, and *Lindisfarenaea* in 890. It could mean 'the island of the people who travelled to and from Lindis', the name for north Lincolnshire.

I have been lifted above the clouds of morning,
Slanted over landfall with shafts of evening light,
Breathed in salt-splashed air
That sparkles haloes to the shattered sun.
A gentle, flattened coastline spread below a wash of cloud,
Is broken by an island deep as it is tall.
There is a boat that hangs in space,
Masted with birch, with silken sails,
Drenched with a rainbow of hope.

Lindis is left far behind.
The call of a gull, wave-beat and lull,
Wreckage of lives resisting the pull
Of the sea from the shore are no more.

This silent water hides the thrust and pulse
Of purple jellyfish around a broken base
Of basalt columns growing in the sea.
A Viking's bloody axe pursues
The eager eyes of missionary priests.
A sacred script with inlaid gold
Moves among drowned hands of weed.

Above the moonrise and the leap of stars,
The kestrel's stillness, curving curlew's flight,
A crucifix of cormorant drying out its wings,
Lies the lost heart of Lindisfarne.

The land of Lindis lies somewhere
Beyond the prow that now I point
Away from land, away from all security
Of places with a name.
The same now
As it was when travellers came
To name
The isle of Lindisfarne.

The 'Lordly Strand' of Northumberland is renowned for stretches of sand and rocky outcrops, even when industry has encroached. Ross Links and Bamburgh are particularly good beaches for those who like sand, but there are places south of Craster, such as Rumbling Kern (churn), where the rock formations are rich in varied layers, twisted shapes and fossils, where the sea roars into gaps and throws spray into the air. Whinstone cliffs are in marked contrast to the sedimentary limestone and sandstone pavements. Columnar basalt at Bamburgh and Dunstanburgh has crystallised over the horizontal strata to form a nesting place for hundreds of birds that streak the cliffs with their droppings and fill the air with their cries. Faults crack and bend rocks; at Dunstanburgh on the path north from the castle to Embleton there is a lovely anticline, followed by dark rounded boulders thrown up in a great storm that closed what served as a harbour for shallow-draught boats. The beach is overlooked by Easter Island statue-like shapes at the edge of the whinstone cliff where the Lilburn tower stands. From a distance the castle towers are like a hand reaching from the earth.

There is so much beauty here, but the picture changes the further south one travels beyond Alnmouth, Warkworth and Amble. At Lynemouth it was not the Alcan aluminium smelters that offended, but a loophole in the law has allowed tonnes of waste to be tipped on the pretext that it was for road-building, a practice graphically exposed by television at the time. Druridge Bay has been a centre of environmental protest when so much of its sand was being extracted commercially, and later when it was being considered as a burial place for nuclear waste or as the site of a nuclear power station. People must live by what they earn; coal mining once provided a living for thousands and created vibrant communities; the last deep pit at *Ellington* may have gone, but opencast mining continues. Opencast creates fewer problems long-term, as sites are filled up again, but the closure of deep mines creates problems of polluted water seeping into streams and rivers and maintains the threat of land subsidence. Wind power has made a bid as alternative energy at Blyth, but although everyone talks about the need for renewable energy it is often opposed if it directly affects residents. It is clear that the north of England, having

Rumbling Kern sedimentary rock formation.

Dunstanburgh Castle from the south.

lost so much of its industrial base, has drastically to rethink its future. Meanwhile the old lingers on, deliberately in the case of Woodhorn Colliery, saved as a museum.

Coal was the basis of northern industrial supremacy. It was of high quality, and the challenge to extract and transport it resulted in quality engineering. The first horse-drawn wagonway was constructed at Bedlington at the time of the accession of James I. Already in the eighteenth-century mining technology was well advanced for extracting coal, pumping out water and transporting the coal to the ports, particularly on the Tyne. The coming of the railways accelerated the whole process, so that south-east Northumberland became one of the most important mining areas in Britain. Small collieries catered for local needs.

Coal production soared with the increased demand in the nineteenth century, mines were sunk deeper, accidents happened, and there were disasters. Port facilities were improved. Whole new communities came into being such as Bedlington in 1840 and Ashington in 1860. The northern coalfield had a quarter of the mines and workers in Britain, and the explosion in population brought a housing boom too. At Ashington we see the well-designed terraces that met this need. Today in the Woodhorn Colliery Museum we see an aspect of life there: the great achievements of the group of painters who earned their livings in that community and who have captured so well the spirit of the place. Brick and tile manufacture was an offshoot of mining. Those who owned the land under which minerals lay grew rich, and released land for building to become richer. With the population increase the demand for gas, electricity and water made it essential to put them under public control. Recently, and perhaps a little ironically, the largest enterprise for supplying water was the building of the giant Kielder reservoir (1975–81), the completion of which coincided with a decline in the demand for it. There has been talk of 'exporting' water to drought-stricken areas to the south, especially when Global Warming takes more effect.

At Lynemouth and Ellington there was a symbiotic relationship between coal and aluminium smelting, for which bauxite has to be imported through the port of Blyth. The Alcan smelter came into production in 1972. Now it is closed.

Seaton Sluice is testimony to an earlier enterprise, when Sir Ralph Delaval built a pier there before 1676 and Sir John Hussey Delaval increased the potential of the harbour by having a canal cut through the rock 275 m long, 9.1 m wide and 15.8 m deep. Coal, salt and bottles were among the exports, but the enterprise was short lived. As a symbol of Delaval power Admiral George Delaval built a mansion at Seaton Delaval, employing Sir John Vanbrugh as the architect, from 1718–29. It is very impressive, with the square hall flanked by rectangular wings facing into a hollow square. There is something very sombre about the blackened sandstone, and it is a powerful, formidable building. It has had many calamities, including fires in 1752 and 1822, but it has now been rescued and is again open to the public.

Woodhorn Colliery, now a county museum and archive centre.

Druridge Bay.

Opencast coalmining at Stobswood.
(*Gordon Tinsley*)

NEWBIGGIN

The town has much to say about the history of the county. Founded as 'the new building' in the twelfth century, it is situated on a large curving bay, looking out towards power stations, a windfarm and other industrial structures of the coast further south. It has a long, towered and steepled church of St Bartholomew detached from the village, situated high on a headland overlooking the sea. Like Holy Island and Hartlepool, there is a strong suggestion that it could have begun its life as a monastic settlement. Today the west tower and its fourteenth-century spire rise far above land and sea, and can be seen for miles.

The tower is tall, straight, unbuttressed and multi-period, but 'hints and allegations' are not enough to make it Saxon. The rest looks from the outside like a long rectangular box, relatively modern, but hiding inside a very complex architectural history. The east end, facing a host of modern headstones (mostly black with unconventional logos and lettering), contains recycled medieval grave slabs. Inside are some magnificent cross slabs of the same period. The nave is long and narrow, incorporating some twelfth-century masonry. Part of the chancel is thirteenth and fourteenth century. At one time the aisles had gone and the chancel had no roof, so what we see today is a restoration. The graveyard is well worth a visit, partly to see changes in the way we regard the dead, and partly to see the effect of weathering on sandstone.

Above: Newbiggin by the Sea.

Right: Newbiggin church tower.

The sea front has all that has happened to architecture recently. Gone has the uniformity that rows of terraced houses brought with them; the DIY movement has made it possible for people to re-style their house fronts, so rendering, pebble-dash, false stone fronts and double glazed windows have created a new look. The traditional 'main street' facilities have deteriorated, leaving little shops with tatty fronts trying to live in the shadow of superstores within easy car-reach. The pubs appear distinctly 'industrial' in their designs and names, as though they have no wish to change. The local council altered the look of the main street by the use of different coloured sets and paving stones. The town is a compact society with its own identity. Pigeon lofts and allotments clutter to the west just off the sea front. Horses are tethered on available grass. The tennis courts are, like so many others, now useless, but the fenced bowling green is still operational. The sea defences have been strengthened. The promontory on which the church stands has a caravan park.

The 'Cresswell Arms' is noted publicly as the last pub before Norway, and the Baker-Cresswell squirrels, found in the north of the county away from the traditional Cresswell power base are here displayed on the pub sign.

Tucked away behind the seafront is that vital part of working class life, the Wesleyan chapel, built in 1844 for the small fishing community. There is a Mechanics Institute with red brick, sandstone facings, a blue slate roof and a turret on a corner of the main street. It is still possible to pick out the fishermens' cottages, but other buildings heralded a new prosperity when the demand for leisure included seaside holidays, with an exodus from the large towns in the summer.

Today the demand for leisure facilities has become greater and more sophisticated, but whereas in the past three-quarters of the people were dependent on coal mining, there is need to diversify. Newbiggin may have been given a new lease of life in the thirteenth century as the 'new' building, but nearby Cramlington was established as a New Town to take 60,000 people.

Villages and towns visibly retain some of their history, and there is now a greater awareness that the past can disappear unless it is planned otherwise. At Cresswell, once a spring where watercress grew, a fifteenth century tower of three storeys has survived. Around it is an estate village of the early nineteenth Century, but the hall was pulled down in 1937. It is a quiet place, with horses tethered between it and the sea.

Sea ports like Blyth are undergoing yet another change since the expansion of industry, such as windfarm equipment manufacture, has given new opportunities.

MORPETH

Morpeth is now the centre of county administration, with the building of County Hall from 1979–82. It has attractive rubbed-brick reliefs depicting Northumberland history. The town grew up at a crossing place on the River Wansbeck, its name meaning a path across the moor, or wasteland. Its castles and church lie on the south side of the river, and its market centre to the north.

Blyth, a port further south.

A striking difference between the architecture of this town and other old established ones is that it has more brick buildings in its centre; a fire in the seventeenth century led to rebuilding the smaller houses in brick, a fashion that continued in the eighteenth century. Today it has expanded into a number of low-density housing estates that cater for those who work locally and those who wish to commute. It retains some attractive old buildings such as its old bridge, tower and the Chantry, the latter being an information centre and a museum of Northumbrian pipes.

Some people want to build a new County Hall in Ashington—a controversial plan.

7

Scarpland: Edlingham

A concerted effort was made in the eighteenth and nineteenth centuries to build a new network of roads, beginning with the trunk routes in Northumberland. One of the earliest was a turnpike road from Hexham to Alnmouth, known as the Alemouth Corn Road; it respected field boundaries except when the land was unenclosed, which accounts for alternating winding and straight stretches. Along the turnpikes were tollhouses and mileposts. At Corby's Letch, near Edlingham, a bridge was constructed specifically in 1754 for the road. When the railways were constructed this road-building programme began to wind down, and control of the roads passed to highway authorities. Today at Edlingham the railway is abandoned but the road is frequently used.

The part of the road that runs from Alnwick to Rothbury crosses the main A697 from Morpeth to Coldstream at Newmoor crossroads. That is an interesting spot, for within a few hundred metres are two old roads no longer in use: the Roman Devil's Causeway and the coaching road from the south to Scotland that lies south-west of the A697. The north-south route follows the course of the Millstone Burn, which links a low-lying area leading to the coastal plain with the sandstone ridges and Cheviot Hills in the north. The coach road, still a well- defined public track, at its highest point passes through scattered woodland, fields enclosed by walls, and is carried across a burn by a culvert reputed to be haunted by a black boar. The remains of a stone inn are now used as a store and enclosure. There is much dark green bottle glass just under the surface, probably the remains of provisions for travellers, for here horses were changed. It is a very odd place, with an atmosphere that many find uncomfortable, next to the wild moorland that stretches away to Cragside. It is sometimes known as Rimside, though this applies to the moorland and forest immediately to the north. The old road runs on to Whittingham and Glanton (a lookout place) via Thrunton Woods, an area of forest walks that lead to good views of the Vale of Whittingham.

Prehistoric people may have used a different route, for rocks on which they pecked their motifs 'sign the land' in a north-east/south-west direction, as we shall see.

The Fell sandstone scarp that runs from Alnwick to Newmoor has one of the most exciting views in the county. To the north-west of its line is lower, undulating

The old carriageway at Rimside, connecting Newcastle with Edinburgh.

Edlingham church, castle and viaduct.

land where the village of Edlingham is situated. There is a Norman church, rig and furrowed ploughed fields, demesne lands, an old 'pillow mound' of a rabbit warren (at a time when rabbits were sparse enough for people to encourage), and sand quarries overlooked by a Roman road that runs north to a flattened Roman fort at Learchild and a Romano-British farmstead. It has a castle that, when I first visited it, was a ruined leaning tower packed with rubble and pigeon droppings, with most of its northern range of buildings covered with a green mound and trees. It is rare for a castle to be excavated on such a scale, but the whole plan was uncovered between 1978–82; a sequence of buildings that tells us much about how this castle developed as a defence and a residence.

From a moated enclosure it became a large hall house built by Sir William Felton in the last five years of the thirteenth century. It was a two-storey block with octagonal towers at each corner, within which there were spiral staircases. On the north was an external stair to the first storey.

The cracked tower, which is such an attraction for artists, was added in the mid-fourteenth century, having three storeys with diagonal buttresses and 'bartizans' on top. It is remarkably rich in decoration inside, with ornate fireplaces and arches that spring from capitals decorated with heads. Here I was introduced to the term 'joggling" by a builder in one of my classes: curved notches with corresponding grooves that fit the top stones of the fireplaces together like a simple jigsaw puzzle.

Corby's Crags sandstone scarp.

There is a window seat on the ground floor facing south. Contemporary with this is a curtain wall built with a barbican gatehouse in the north-west. Between the gate and the hall house and tower is a cobbled courtyard and a kitchen range.

What happened to the plundered stone? Some is not hard to find, as close by there is a late nineteenth-century railway viaduct supported on pillars that appear to have old stone bases. The viaduct used to carry the railway from Alnwick to Cornhill, still traceable in many parts, with some elegant now-converted stations that show just how good railway architecture was. Here the track curves out of its cuttings and is carried over the bridge, a thing of beauty.

Church, castle and viaduct make a picture rich in interest, with a background of scarpland on which the domed rock shelter of Corby's Crags is visible.

THE CORBY'S CRAGS ROCK SHELTER

I was at work in Alnwick castle one late afternoon when a local teacher brought some small pieces of prehistoric pottery rim to me that he had found under a rock overhang. I went with him at once to the site, which is a natural dome of sandstone with a slit-like space underneath, As the sun was setting the oblique rays picked out in shadow a large artificial basin surrounded by a groove, with a channel leading from its centre down the rock. The dome itself had been cut through, and steps made to carry the path down to the shelter. This boundary, marked with S and P cut into the rock, divided Percy from Swinburne lands. There were signs of millstone extraction. A fence continued the boundary away from the rock up the hill, where there is a collection of boulders that could have been part of a monument. Below the rock shelter was a standing stone five metres away, and another further down the hill. Between this and the road was an Iron Age enclosure of two ditches and walls, partly obscured by birch trees, with large defensive stones piled on the scarp edge overlooking the road. Around the dome were many filled-in bell pits, used for superficial extraction of coal. Since then a stray find of an early Bronze Age arrowhead ('equal barb and tang') has been made.

It used to surprise me that such things had passed unnoticed before, but not any more. The view from the dome overlooks the junction of the Edlingham Burn and the Swinhope Burn. To the east and north-east the higher ground cuts off the view, but to the west over Lumbey Law farm, Coe Crags and Thrunton Crags stand out, with the Cheviot Hills visible behind them. To the north is a series of sandstone scarps and slopes, with Ros Castle prominent on the far horizon. What a place to live in, and what a place to be buried in; for those small pieces of pottery were the rim of an early Bronze Age 'food vessel' some four thousand years old, containing a cremation.

I excavated the floor of the rock shelter, where there was a compact but shallow covering of earth that contained a remarkable mixture of artefacts from about eight thousand years ago to the present. The first to use the shelter were nomadic Middle Stone Age (Mesolithic) hunters who chipped their tiny blades and arrow

Corby's Crags rock shelter.

points there, leaving over 30 fragments. Four thousand years ago, people who had by now developed arable farming but who still hunted and herded animals chose the place to bury one of their folk by digging into the floor, prising out a triangular-shaped piece of stone, placing it over an upright pot which held the cremation, then covering it over so effectively that no one knew it was there. The same people may have been responsible for the motif on top of the shelter and for a picked groove on the floor that runs towards the burial spot. Although the base of the pot had suffered from its hole acting as a sump, I was able to lift the pot and its surrounding soil for excavation at the Museum of Antiquities at Newcastle. It was an attractive vessel, with three lines of grain impressions running round it, and from the rim to shoulder were lugs around the pot at 5 cm intervals, each decorated and stuck on, not pinched.

What must surely have been noticed prior to 1975 was that an armchair had been cut into the solid rock of the overhang, and little ledges made on either side. This period of use is explained by finds from the material in the floor: three stems of clay pipes and a pipe bowl, green glass, white glass, a decorated tea cup or bowl, a knife with a metal blade and wooden handle, various pieces of iron, and two pieces of thin wheel-turned pot. Other clues to the use of the shelter came from notches in the rock and a low wall built outside it: the shelter would have had an additional screen, people such as shepherds or bell-pit workers could shelter there, sit in the rock chair, put their 'bait' and bottles on the ledges, have their meal, and enjoy a good view, oblivious of the dead man at their feet.

We excavated the base of the large standing stone on the slopes down from the shelter; we expected the stone to be slotted in a hole, but it was wedged by smaller stones under its flat base. The prehistoric enclosure was recorded by Ordnance Survey, and is now on the maps. Below it by the road is a small waterfall. There must surely be more discoveries to be made, and another example came to light at Lemmington Wood when Irene and Ian Hewitt were relocating a panel of rock art; they discovered that runes, extremely rare, had been carved on the same outcrop. Consultation with specialists suggested that they were part of a sacred text, and that their meaning was either the Old English verb *laefen*, to leave or leave behind, or the Old English noun *laf*, meaning a remnant or a relic. An alternative is that they are Old Norse, from the noun *lof*, meaning praise or permission, or from *laf*, meaning bread or sustenance.

The scarp runs south-west to an outcrop of sandstone called Caller Crags, where there are many natural strange shapes formed by erosion, a perched, naturally cupped stone and a small cave facing a terrace. On the back of the vertical outcrop is a cluster of cup marks, a Neolithic legacy. Following this outcrop southwards parallel to the Millstone Burn we have recently located a flat panel of cups and rings on a path that leads to more spectacular marked sites at Snook Bank. When the ground was ploughed for forestry plantations, flints came to the surface. Millstone cutting may have destroyed some archaeology in the area.

To return to the village of Edlingham, between the castle and the church of John the Baptist a large medieval grave slab was found, and is now in the church along

A basin and groove on the top of the rock-shelter

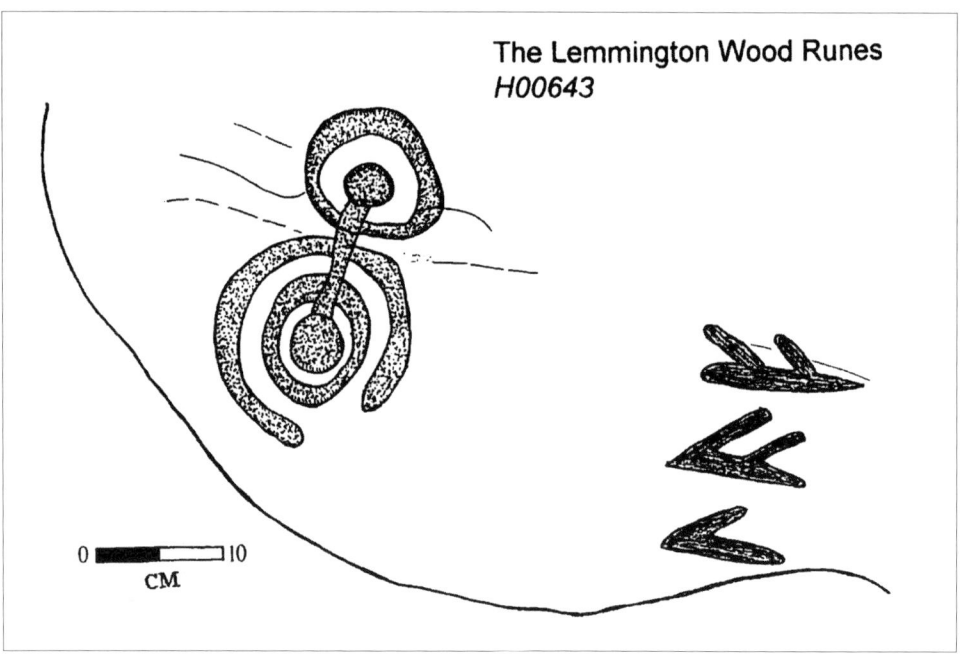

A unique combination of cup and ring marks and runes, Lemmington Hill.

with a pre-Conquest cross-shaft. The church has a conspicuously massive tower with tiny windows, and this may have doubled as a defence during Border raids. This is later than the nave, door and chancel arch. The church has benefited hugely from the care and time that local people have put into it. It is not only attractive, but its history is lovingly displayed and its large graveyard well maintained.

I conclude this little portrait with a poem that stemmed from here:

Autumn Gold

This valley holds the melting point of gold.
Here, at this year's end, poised
Above a sandstone scarp
With fretted water pouring from its cheeks,
We tremble on the edge of silence
And the hovering kestrel's path of time.
Below, a shattered castle keep
Blends with the shadows of green earth
As sunlight slowly strokes each tree and field.
A subtle shift of texture threads the cooling air
Among the gentle fall of leaves,

Caller Crags: an outstanding sandstone formation.

Spinning of winged seeds, or sigh of brittle pine.
But far beyond the urgent change that dying bracken at our feet foretells,
The rounded Cheviots snuggle closer to warm clouds,
While all the space between is indistinct, Simmering:
A crucible of westering sun
Still glowing gold, dark green and brown,
With flames of scarlet licking round.

The store of summer drains away
To leave an aching sadness
For the richness that was there.
Cold realisation of our loss
Throbs slowly through the current of our blood;
We touch the rock for reassurance
That next year will be the same,
And after that…and after that…
Who knows?
Our bodies cry inside, 'Stay, stay. Come back, come back.'
Yet even as we watch, the sun-shift and the lengthened shadows
Drag away the hope
That we can catch and keep the feeling and the sight
For ever.
Soon, all this valley will be drained of light.

Edlingham valley.

8

Power and Place:
Lord Armstrong and Cragside

When I was headteacher at Rothbury Middle School my staff agreed to use a week of the school term for the whole school to have their work centred on nearby Cragside, a large house visible among the trees across the Coquet valley from the school. Sometimes curriculum can be fragmentary, and there is a tendency to compartmentalise subjects, thus inhibiting the wholeness of learning. Here was an opportunity to integrate everything into one theme: the life and times of one of the most important figures in British industry. Lord Armstrong represents the kind of Victorian enterprise that transformed landscapes and industry to make Britain 'The Workshop of the World'. It was also an opportunity to involve not only the community in the process, but also outside bodies such as The National Trust and the County Record Office. Such schemes commit the staff to enormous quantities of extra work. The first step was to acquaint everyone, through a leaflet, with the life of Lord Armstrong and what he achieved.

William Armstrong, with a traditional Border name, was born in Newcastle in 1810, the son of a successful corn merchant who eventually became mayor. At that time the city was for some a very exciting place to live in, but for others a place of long hours and bad working conditions. The war with France was in full swing; by the time of Waterloo (1815) George Stephenson of Wylam had made his first reliable steam locomotive. Armstrong from his early youth had a very inquisitive mind and enjoyed being busy. He could think widely and with great concentration. He said:

> However high we climb in the pursuit of knowledge we shall still see heights above us, and the more we extend our view, the more conscious we shall be of the immensity of what lies beyond.

Shades of Alexander Pope and his 'Alps upon Alps arise'. There was plenty of commercial and industrial activity to feed his mind, plenty to extend his horizons.

As a boy he was not well, and was sometimes taken to Rothbury on holiday, where he developed a keen interest in fishing. When he became rich and famous this deeply embedded enjoyment of the Coquetdale landscape influenced his choice of place for the building of his house.

Cragside: a bridge built as part of the architectural project.

Activity in Newcastle clubs provided an opportunity for men of science, literature and commerce to meet; lateral thinking, problem solving and invention were encouraged. Even when he was practising law, his first career, Armstrong became interested in waterpower and designed an engine. In 1823 at Watson's Engineering Works in Newcastle he made a hydraulic motor that produced 5 hp from Newcastle's water mains. He became interested in electricity produced by steam forced from a boiler. He made the steam boiler of wrought iron on insulated glass legs and called it his 'evaporating apparatus' and later his 'hydro-electric machine'. He became famous when his machines produced spectacularly long electric sparks!

It was at Elswick on the banks of the Tyne west of Newcastle that he developed hydraulics, based on feeding water through pipes to build up enough pressure to drive machines, and applied it to industry. Public health demanded a good water supply, and in 1845 he put forward a plan to the City Council to use water mains also to generate power for the operation of cranes on the quayside. He introduced his first crane once he had the go-ahead for his scheme. At Cragside the 'Ram House' demonstrates this power, working through a chain and pulley to lift and lower weights that put pressure on the head of water.

He could then afford to leave legal practice, and in 1847 he founded *W. G. Armstrong and Company* at Elswick. From lifts and cranes he moved on to use hydraulics to open and close dock gates. If the water mains could not produce enough pressure he built towers and pumped the water up to an artificial reservoir to get the right pressure. His *hydraulic accumulator* had a heavy weight raised by a pumping engine acting as a ram to force water up the pipes. He began to apply his skills to printing presses, machinery for coal and lead mines, and he built bridges. He exported machinery, and when the Royal Navy changed from sail to steam power it brought more business. At the time of the building of the first Cragside house, Armstrong was famous.

War and the need for weapons brought him more money; a mine that could be detonated underwater by electricity, for example. His greatest invention was the breech-loading gun, and his first piece of artillery is on show in the Newcastle Discovery Museum. Soon he was equipping battleships with guns. His guns were exported all over the world, against competition, and one wonders whether he lost any sleep knowing that he had equipped protagonists in the same war. His artillery, though, gained him a knighthood, and he gave the patents to the country.

CRAGSIDE

After 1864 he began to share the management of the Elswick works with others; he concentrated on building Cragside and on Natural History and Scientific research. In 1863 he took his first holiday since 1847, went to Rothbury and decided to build himself a house, in the year when being elected President of the British Association for the Advancement of Science and organising its conference made him tired enough to take a holiday. He turned to what he called 'Planting, building, electrical and scientific research'.

> I believe I first came to Rothbury as a babe in arms, and my earliest recollections consist of paddling in the Coquet, gathering pebbles from its gravel beds, and climbing amongst the rocks on the Crag. For many years I annually visited Rothbury with my parents and under well-known celebrities I learned to fish. The Coquet then became to me a river of pleasure … a source of enjoyment to me all through my life. As a boy, my health was delicate, and more than once an apparently incurable cough was quickly removed by coming to Rothbury, and it had not been for its curative effect there would have been no Cragside nor any Lord Armstrong.

He knew the site well that he chose and 'decided to build for myself a small house in the neighbourhood for occasional visits in the summer time'.

His plan developed beyond the modest house that he began to build in 1863 and was complete by 1866. The stone was quarried on the spot, and the excavated part formed the site of the house. The landscape was largely rough, poor moorland with outcrops of sandstone, crossed by burns that emptied into the Coquet. The house was a two-storey lodge, and whilst it was being built he and his wife lived in the miller's house in a similar way to people who today live in caravans during the building of their new houses. There are pictures of this early house, many copies of which found their way into the school display. It had a central water tower with a pointed roof that was echoed by gables around the house. There were mullioned

Above and below: Cragside house.

windows, with good views where they faced the valley. The roof was pantiled. Armstrong and his wife had experience of landscaping at their house at Jesmond Dene, and used this to good effect.

The house that we see today incorporates the smaller one, but it exhibits a variety of styles. There is good local stone, gothic arches, mullioned windows and some neo-Tudor black and white timber framing as decoration. There are twisted barley sugar chimneys. The architect Norman Shaw was mainly responsible for this development or transformation between 1870–1885. There were later additions such as the billiard room extension.

Inside there is a wealth of social interest and architectural variety, though it is not to everyone's taste. There is, for example, a quite awful massive ornate Italian marble fireplace in the Drawing Room, yet leading to it, via some attractive William Morris glass, is an elegant long gallery with arch braced roof trusses. This was chosen by one class from the school as a base for entertaining visitors during the 'week', and included the tribute that one of Armstrong's men made to him on the success of the gun that brought them so much work:

The Armstrong Gun, the Armstrong Gun,
What a wonderful thing is the Armstrong Gun,
Sir William's invention astonished them all,
Wi' a bolt for a shot instead of a ball.

Nae spungin' or ramin' or servin' the vent—
Such things are no' needed to serve its intent.
In a neat little chamber breech end of the bore
Place the powder and shot and away let it roar.

Then there's fuses, they're said, such wonders I tell,
They 'splode the bolt shells when it pleases themsel's
It's short range or long range, it's a' the same thing,
Jest set 'em—they're true to the secret spring.

The gunboats hae now lost their glory and pride,
For wor gun sends its bolts slapbang thro' its side,
Neither iron or oak can resist its ava,
When it vomits them forth frae its terrible jaws.

So success to Sir William, and long may it thrive!
May his days be as glad as the bees in his hive,
Wi' his greatness of mind, he's the patience of Job,
He's now made a gun that can conquer the Globe!

The building of Cragside coincided with, or was the result of, a movement away from his industrial base, as he became less involved in running it. In 1882 he amalgamated his firm and a shipbuilder's so that it became Sir W. G. Armstrong, Mitchell and Company. The remaining years of the century saw his superiority in armaments manufacture and in the production of Ironclad ships. Armstrong's made half of the Japanese fleet that defeated the Russian navy in 1905.

There are still relics in the house of how it became a focus of distinguished visitors, many from abroad, who came to buy arms. The King of Siam and the Shah of Persia visited in 1889, and the Crown Prince of Afghanistan in 1895. The local people would have remembered particularly, though, the visit of the Prince of Wales and his family, who travelled by train in 1884 to Rothbury, and were met at the station by a carefully graded reception committee including the leading local citizens. The village was treated to an impressive display of fireworks that was fully reported by the Press.

He became Baron Armstrong of Cragside in 1887. He gave large sums of money, which he could well afford, to charities and to institutions in Newcastle. In Northumberland he will be well remembered for the rebuilding of Bamburgh castle, which he bought in 1894.

The people who could see Cragside either from the inside or outside were impressed by the technology built into it. His large enterprises, such as the building of the Swing Bridge at Newcastle and the installation of hydraulic machinery in the Tower Bridge, London, were reflected on a smaller scale in his house and grounds. Out of 1,700 acres of land at Cragside, there are 76 acres of water made by damming burns and building lakes. The first was Tumbleton Lake in 1866 on the Debdon Burn,

Cragside: a dam, the basis of a hydro-electric scheme.

used to power a hydraulic ram, which forced water up to the house and grounds. In 1870 Debdon Lake was made higher up, followed by Nelly's Moss lakes higher still. The water was used to power the electricity generator, a sawmill, the house's hydraulic passenger and service lifts and the kitchen's roasting spit. In Cragend farm two large silage pits each have one-tonne masoned stones operated hydraulically to crush the grass in the pits, although it is believed that it only worked once —or less. The powerhouse at Burnfoot was used from 1887, and became the source of electricity for the house.

The lighting, installed in 1880 by Joseph Swan, was most spectacular. We take it for granted that when we press a switch the light comes on, but imagine the sense of wonder generated by the first house in the world to have electric light. Armstrong says, 'The brook, in fact, lights the house, and there is no consumption of any material in the process.' Electricity was generated by a turbine about 1,400 m away. It passed along about 2,700 m of thick copper wire encased in wood to complete the circuit and could light 45 lamps. 'For this number of lamps, 6 horse-power proves to be amply sufficient', he wrote in 1881, and described how his library had eight lamps, four clustered in one globe. He liked the softness of the light produced, which was the same as about 25 candles per lamp:

> It is perfectly steady and noiseless. It is free from harsh glare and shadows. It casts no ghastly hue on the countenance, and shows everything in true colours . . . In short, nothing can be better than this light for domestic use.

In daytime he sometimes used the same dynamo and generator to power a second machine that drove a sewing machine. In 1887 he had a permanent hydroelectric powerhouse built at Burnfoot, the water coming from Nelly's Moss lakes, and installed batteries as a back-up.

The Prince of Wales' visit was an opportunity to show off this technology; the rooms in the house blazed with light, and this was accompanied by the firework displays arranged by a specialist from London and a huge bonfire lit on the Simonside hills opposite. Not only would all the local people and visitors have been impressed, but also the locals would have been thanking Armstrong for creating so many jobs for them. Think of the thousands of evergreens and heathers that had to be planted by hand, or the work of building miles of carriageways and paths, or the construction of dams for lakes, of the erection of a single span iron bridge 150 feet (45 m) long, and we can see what a large labour force was involved. This is reflected in the census returns, a great source of information that the children used in their project. They found out about people who lived in Rothbury and about the workers employed in Cragside itself. We see the exercise of great power, of vision, wealth, knowledge and of organisation, all of which Armstrong had.

There are issues that have concerned and divided people, such as the rightness or wrong of war, since recorded time. Aristophanes, concerned with the apparently endless and futile wars in ancient Greece, suggested in his comedy 'Lysistrata' that if women withheld themselves from men as a weapon, the warriors would stop

Portrait of Lord Armstrong by
Mary Lemmon Walker.

fighting. Henry V in Shakespeare's celebration of nationalism and kingship, is faced with his responsibility when all the legs and arms chopped off in battle unite to accuse him of their fate. The decision to bomb Hiroshima and Nagasaki and the spread of nuclear weapons means that there is no guarantee that such weapons will keep the peace. The late Robin Cook tried to put the case for 'Moral Foreign Policy', but the export of arms to dubious regimes goes ahead. The dilemma that we face when we try to assess Lord Armstrong's place in history is not based on a dead issue. The continuing interest in the First World War, for example in the popularity of Pat Barker's novels, the study of attitudes, campaigns and the military mind, is concerned with a catastrophe that happened 14 years after Armstrong's death, in which he contributed considerably to the means. There are familiar arguments put forward to justify our armaments industry: progress in arms technology helps to protect British interests; if we don't make arms, someone else will; if we stop making them, unemployment will rise.

Here we have a genius, generally a mild-mannered man who did not smoke, who drank only moderately, and hated swearing. He liked children, but was childless. He had a concentrated mind, a capacity for hard work and a great imagination. A Liberal Unionist, he had no desire to go into politics, but felt so passionately anti-Home Rule for Ireland that he allowed himself to be put up for election to Parliament, only to be defeated after a low-key campaign. His stance was: 'I declare myself the decided opponent of any scheme which may lead to the disintegration of the British Empire, or involve the desertion of the loyal party in Ireland, whose members are veiled by the terrorism which prevents the free assertion of individual opinion when opposed to the dominant faction of the country.' He represented Rothbury on Northumberland County Council from 1889–92, but his interest in politics was lukewarm.

William Armstrong supported charities, gave money for building hospitals and convalescent homes, encouraged the building of schools and made education available for his workforce in the enormous complex of factories and domestic sites at Elswick. Yet he opposed the introduction of a nine-hour day put to him politely by his workers' representatives, which resulted in the shut-down of his works and the migration of about 6,000 workers to other areas and jobs; he only agreed when it was obvious that the loss of orders would cost more than agreeing to his workers' demands. The Elswick community expanded from 3,539 in 1851 to 27,000 in 1871, and the men worked six days a week at 10 hours a day. Their life expectancy was very low, and few reached 40 years of age. Until the strike, labour relations had been good, but their requests were replied to through 'the most obnoxious firm of solicitors that could have been chosen, the solicitors of the Conservative Association'. An attempt was made to bring in engineers from Germany, Denmark, Belgium and Sweden. Although Armstrong was well capable of dealing with legal wrangles and organisation, he did not make a good job of relationships with his men on this occasion.

His interests were encouraged in the rapidly-changing world of the North when enterprise and invention were paramount. He was happier with his inventions than with some of the consequences such as the bitter rivalries with people like Joseph Whitworth of Manchester over armaments, or with the ignorance and entrenched conservatism of the military establishment of Britain. In later life he found some peace and new inspiration at Cragside, but he seems not to have lost his driving force and energy.

What Cragside represents is a monument to his memory, reminding us of the industrial base on which his fortune was built, the tastes of someone designing his own house and grounds, and his eye to the future, for he knew that he would not see the fruition of his work in planting those thousands of trees, shrubs and heathers. Fortunately the responsibility for maintenance and restoration of this fascinating house and grounds belongs to the National Trust. It has enabled the people of the Rothbury area and their children to ponder awhile on another age through a great visual aid. The staff of Dr Thomlinson's Middle School was able to use this unique resource, and it is now used in a similar way by other schools.

The project took place in April 1988, and involved many parents and a group of post-graduate education students from the Institute of Education, Newcastle University.

Why Cragside? Because it's there. The house reflects Victorian inventiveness, was the original concept of one man, and employed other talents to realise it. His life is a microcosm of an age.

Its establishment had a great effect on the surrounding area. It provides an excellent opportunity to focus the work of children on one geographical area, and integrates

A small selection of things used in Lord Armstrong's time by local people, brought into school for display.

many parts of the curriculum. Thus the study of water and water power, hydraulics and electricity, social divisions reflected in the 'upstairs–downstairs' organisation of a big Victorian house, the transformation of the landscape and its vegetation, analysis of the census, examination of what people of the time had in their homes, such as samplers and postcards, what they wore and what they ate, what games they played, how they entertained themselves or were entertained, why there was a railway but there isn't one now—the possibilities are many. Among the objects brought in for display was a souvenir Cragside cheese dish made in Austria, an interesting discovery. Objects such as these provided a visual history of the time, so important to children's learning. Copies of newspapers were particularly useful, especially those that reported the Prince of Wales' visit and accounts of Armstrong's career.

Drawing attention through the Press to the work done by the school brought a renewed interest in the resource, so we all benefited. Since that project, much more has been done to make Cragside attractive to visitors.

I finish this section with a reflection: on the moorlands that adjoin the Cragside grounds is an area of burial cairns built over four thousand years ago, with a standing stone on the ridge overlooking them. Above a small stream is an arc of stone-based roundhouses of the pre-Roman period, where one stands slightly higher than the others are and detached from them. Pylons stride across the moorland above the bellpit mounds, the places where superficial mining was carried out for coal. Everywhere there are signs of human activities, and each age makes different use of the land. History is about change, and the jet fighters that scream overhead are a reminder of how precarious the present is.

A Prehistoric settlement site overlooked by a standing stone, close to Cragside.

9

Empty Places? Hexhamshire and the Cheviots

There are many areas in Northumberland that appear to be almost empty of people, the higher ground in particular, such as the north eastern Pennines and the Cheviot Hills. This is a relief to those who have little taste for overcrowded urban areas. The emptiness may be offset by a realisation that slight shifts in climate, erosion as a result of the removal of vegetation and fragile topsoil and changes in industrial or farming practice disguise a different and lucrative use of that land in the past.

Some of the signs are obvious. A trip through Hexhamshire to the Cumbrian and Durham borders opens up a world of derelict industry, for a huge amount of lead was produced here. Much of the raw material was mined through 'hushing', a process in which streams were dammed, the build-up of water released, with the exposure of the underlying galena. Other mining goes miles underground, often horizontally to reach the more or less vertical ore deposits. Quarries throw up spoil, still easily visible. Mining 'shops' and working floors where lead ore was crushed and washed in 'buddles' are grown over. On some sites there are the remains of stark, imposing chimneys and linear mounds running uphill to meet them, covering the sandstone flue tunnels. A single chimney and flue at Langley, running from the smelt mill near Langley Castle, stands close to a well-preserved building at the head of a coal mine on the Alston road from Hexham. Some quarrying leaves massive amounts of spoil, but there are other signs of activity: the stone cottages, often in decay, of the lead miners, with their gardens, a valued respite from mines and washing floors and a place to grow food. Communities died when foreign competition closed what used to be Europe's most important mines and smelters. Drove roads, where pack horses carried lead ore, and trackways were reclaimed by nature.

This is largely limestone and sandstone country, a land of curlews, lapwings, small birds and raptors. Limekilns are interspersed with shrunken settlements. Fields, once cultivated for arable, are now pasture. Skyscapes are wide and dramatic, the wind frequently cold and strong, and it is colder in exposed places than in the valleys.

A scene in Hexhamshire. (*From* Memories of Hexhamshire, *by Hilary Kristenson*)

A flue at Catton.

There has been an increasing interest in lead extraction and smelting, not only in the technicalities but also in the communities that did the work. Over the county border, sites like Nenthead and Killhope have been partially cleaned up and displayed, with some light experience of ore washing and access to the mines made possible. Allenheads had the most important mine in Europe, developed particularly in the nineteenth century by the Beaumont/Blackett family with the expertise of that very talented mining engineer Thomas Sopwith, whose voluminous diaries provide an excellent insight into mining engineering. Everything in this reviving settlement bears witness to the success of that community whose buildings include a school, reading room, library and places of worship as well as houses and administrative buildings. There has also been interest shown by researchers into the role of religion in the lives of the lead workers and their families, especially in the success of the nonconformist churches that are so liberally spread across these areas. They reached the parts that the established church failed to reach.

Some of the earliest lead mining that we know was at Blanchland in the fifteenth century. The north Pennine orefield was extensive, and affected the whole of life within its compass. Everywhere we travel we see that much has been destroyed; some is decayed but still visible, and now we have the deliberate attempt to preserve some of what is left. Allendale, with its buildings focused on a large market square, owes much to mining. Before that, some of its history is reflected in many bastles, some incorporated in farm buildings. A garage has been built on the site of the smelt mill, from which three remarkable 'horizontal chimneys' run to the higher

Catton chimneys to which miles of flues made their way.

ground—long flues that took the fumes away acted as condensers that could have particles of lead and silver scraped out of them. This would have been very bad for the lungs of those who had to do it. The chimneys, on Catton Moor, are a symbol of the revived interest in this past, for they have recently been re-pointed and saved from further decay.

Away from high ground, as in parts of Hexhamshire, there is mixed farming and less-harsh conditions. There are plantations of trees, herds of cattle sharing fields with flocks of sheep. Heather moorland is used to breed grouse for shooting, and suicidal pheasants blend with the road surfaces, often joined by rabbits. For those who like more remote places, many of the crumbling small farms and houses have provided an opportunity for renovation, so that people working out of the area have a convenient base. In this way the influx of cash and materials has saved some fine buildings from complete decay. Not all are 'miles from anywhere'.

A good example of judicious restoration is 'The Tenement' at Steel, not far from Hexham, where a most intriguing and unique dwelling has been restored recently. Among the cluster of old houses and farm buildings this house and barn probably began life as a one-storey house with one door and window. It was extended west as a two-storey building with a cross-passage at the west end of the old house. Its roof was a curved structure made of thick crucks, and its doors seem to have been imported from an earlier medieval building. In the later seventeenth century a mullioned window was put in. There was a fireplace at the west end with a domed bread oven, and here was found an intriguing iron cylindrical oven with a hinged cover that dropped forward, the mystery of which we were able to decipher. It was outside when we examined it, and an eroded inscription turned out to read: *England expects every man to do his duty*. At once the identity of the person facing left in the centre, surrounded by a starburst became known: Nelson. It was made in Gateshead. This was part of an alteration; before that in the early eighteenth century a third extension was built with an end stack that included another bread oven. In the last phase a Tudor-arched door was inserted, as you can see in the picture. There always seems to be something new to discover in this county.

The photograph and Peter Ryder's reconstruction drawings show the possible phases of building at the Tenement.

THE CHEVIOT HILLS

The Cheviot Hills are rounded, cut by narrow streams, and not always easily accessible.

There is a particular attraction for walkers in the variety and beauty of scenery. The hills have many small farms and remote well-integrated communities. Forestry, cattle and sheep farming and some arable in the valleys and lower lands are the means of making a living. There is quarrying, notably of the attractive deep pink rock from Biddlestone (technically known as a laccolith). Forestry continues to spread. The land also bears the traces of prehistoric settlements that have been preserved

The Tenement reconstruction (Peter Ryder) and work in progress.

'The Tenement', Steel, phase I.

'The Tenement', Steel, phase II.

Phase III. The house as it may have appeared c.1830.

so well because people no longer wish to live in the same places or farm the land for arable. Small villages favour valleys, leaving the hilltops to their enclosures, ringworks of prehistoric forts, burial cairns and ancient field systems.

Landscape is primarily determined by underlying geology. Although only two areas are to be examined, they have features of the general picture that follows; I have chosen them to represent the rest because they are particularly rich in remains of the past: the Ingram Valley and the Glen Valley.

THE BREAMISH VALLEY

The river Breamish begins life as a number of small streams south and south-east of the Cheviot, many joining at Linhope. The Dunmore and Linhope burns meet at Linhope Spout, a small but exciting little waterfall that gets its name from a pond in a valley. Just north of the junction of these streams is a well-preserved pre-Roman settlement at Greaves Ash (or Grieves Ash); here are enclosures with roundhouse foundations and yards, with a distinctive hollow way leading into the complex. The whole valley is marked on maps with old settlements and field systems, best seen in autumn and winter when the sun is low and when bracken has died off. There are very clear views of the sites from the air. The main river valley twists and broadens out; other smaller streams are separated from the main river by Hartside Hill, which is particularly well-endowed. So is the hill known as Chesters.

Powburn gravel deposits, some the results of hill farming in the past.

The Breamish sweeps around a hill called Brough Law into the Ingram Valley. Overlooking the bend are the prominent stone ramparts of an Iron Age hill fort, the name Brough Law meaning a fortification on a hill. A well-used path leads to the main car park in the valley, passing several small settlements over terraces and rig and furrow systems.

The valley road gives good access to some of the best walking areas in the hills and is accessible for some distance by car, but the road west to Linhope is restricted to traffic. The slopes that flank the valley are made of volcanic andesite, and there are screes on their slopes. The valley floor has deep rig and furrow, and sometimes car owners must wonder what these high ridges are on which they park their cars; in summer the valley becomes a picnic area and playground, but it is possible in a very short time to leave it and enter a world of extensive views and silence.

THE BREAMISH VALLEY ARCHAEOLOGY PROJECT

Like so many other people, I have found the valley not only conveniently accessible but full of interest at all times of the year. It is a fine place for families with young children, as the river is shallow and full of rounded stones that can be made into temporary dams. It is good for those who want to walk great distances, for those who like to rise above the valley and look down on it from a height that is not too demanding to climb. It is a place to breathe clean air and to escape from crowds. For others it has a wealth of visible settlements from the deep past, and a number of intriguing questions about life in the past that can only, perhaps, be answered by excavation.

Why are there so many remains? To which period do they belong? How can some of the history be exposed, preserved and presented to the public?

Paul Frodsham, Northumberland National Park archaeology officer, explained at the time a major archaeology project in the valley:

> We had high expectations of this project which was set up to build on survey work done previously undertaken by the Royal Commission on Historic Monuments. However, the results have exceeded all expectations. It has been a delight to see so many local people getting involved with, and getting experience from, the project. Archaeology is after all about people, and at the end of the day it should be fun.

People have been involved for years in work undertaken by the National Park, the University of Durham and the Northumberland Archaeological Group. Because I have been involved in the work, the following account is based upon my personal experience; the reader must understand that work is still underway and that there are many corrections and different interpretations to be made. Full excavation reports will be published in due course.

Today the focus of settlement is Ingram village and its farms. Since the fourteenth century the real decline in the settlement of the hills began, but the village remained the focus of life. St Michael's church has been considerably changed with much demolishing and rebuilding, but the interior still looks medieval. The earliest part is the eleventh-century tower. There was another settlement at Alnhamsheles in the upper Breamish valley, where there were 20 rectangular buildings. It was in existence in 1265, with 11 tenants in 1314, but was abandoned by about 1550.

The first step of the project was to consult survey work already done. Once excavation began, it was not confined to exposing a structure, but to analysing pollen and carbon samples to tell us something of the environment in the past and how it changed. A particularly important question is: why is it that such extensive arable cultivation was abandoned for pasture? Did the soil lose its fertility? Did the climate change? A search for answers was to produce some unexpected results. The early stages of work concentrated most of the labour force on Turf Knowe; as the name suggests this is a grass-covered hill overlooking the valley from the south. Only a number of boundary walls were visible; some sites chosen for excavation had nothing recorded on them.

One dyke (wall) running south-west from Ingram village towards Ewe Hill and down Chesters Burn proved to be made of boulders, but some parts were made by excavating a ditch. One part pre-dated some of the farming systems; it was probably Romano-British or earlier.

There was nothing of importance marked on Turf Knowe, but a cairn was excavated with spectacular results, for it proved to be a rare 'tri-radial' type, since

From Brough Law to the River Breamish valley floor: a rich archaeological landscape.

recognised elsewhere in the county. It is built of three walls of different-coloured boulders that meet at a point. Between the meeting place of two of these arms was a pit containing cremations in cists; one had been re-dug and a food vessel displaced in order to insert a later cremation with the decayed remains of an iron spear head. This clearly showed that the site had been used by different peoples as a ritual/burial site from 4,000 years ago to the age of iron perhaps over 2,000 years later. Very often we find that many sites in Britain have this extensive continuity. Beside one of the arms of the cairn was a circular pit in which another food vessel had been placed on a flat stone and crushed with the weight of in-filling. There was also a horseshoe-shaped setting of boulders beside another arm of the cairn where charcoal showed that its use had extended into the AD 500s.

A vital part of archaeology is the 'sequencing' of deposits on a site; through this we are able to work out who did what. I was particularly involved with the excavation of the pit with the three cists and cremations, already exposed, to see whether there were any further indications of the sequence of deposits. Much of archaeology is hard, routine work, in which very little that is exciting is found, but the unexpected is always ready to happen. Take this pit, for example. A hole dug in the ground here is not so easy to define as one would imagine, for the disturbed sub-soil has the same ingredients as the 'natural' undisturbed soil, a brash made up of shattered bits of stone. When the disturbed soil is put back into a hole it may no longer look disturbed. In trying to define the edges of this pit, we encountered a lump of material out of which the top of a pot showed in section; it was so loose that we simply pulled the whole pot out gently before it fell out on its own. It turned out to be a food vessel of a rather plain type that had been displaced by those people who chose the same pit to bury a cremation in a cist with a spear head, perhaps even using the same cist. It is moments like this that add to the excitement of excavation, and reward hours of patient trowelling when little else is revealed. There are moments in a dig when the whole team comes to watch something like this happen.

The techniques that we use today are far removed from those of Canon Greenwell; in a letter dated 1847 he describes a rather bleak and bizarre occasion when he opened a barrow near Chollerton in the Hexham area. He found two bodies, one in an urn, sadly decayed and broken and the other unurned body in a central cist. The snow was six inches deep and the wind high. He examined the cist by candle light, and in a letter to a friend he says 'the scene was a very picturesque one, the workmen standing around in the partial light, some fine old bushes waving around us, and myself on my knees, with a candle held in front of me, discussing the mouldering remains.'

To continue with modern excavation: down the hill away from this cairn, beside a boundary wall, excavations revealed buried soils with a complex arable use, capped by an enigmatic stone structure. These farming systems respected the stone and ditched boundary. The cairn lay away from and above this mundane activity.

When the third season of excavation turned to a new focus on another small hill, lower than the first, an important discovery was made. What appeared rather featureless, with some hints of scattered stone, was a large roughly circular cairn

Discovery of a Food Vessel that had been ejected from a Bronze Age cist in prehistoric times.

Turf Knowe Cairn: unknown until the excavation.

built on a platform. An area much larger than the cairn kerb was excavated, and in this flints from Mesolithic (Middle Stone Age) times appeared with later Neolithic and early Bronze Age flints, so rare in the Cheviots. Such a scatter meant that for up to 8,000 years ago people had used the site, possibly in small hunting groups, but the cairn indicates a more settled and intensive use of the area, possibly by early agriculuralists.

The cairn was built of boulders and cobbles, probably collected from fields or from the river, surrounding two cists in the centre. These were not the only burials, for scattered apparently randomly throughout the cairn were cremated bone fragments and broken pottery. At least 17 cremation burials, some in pits, were located outside the cists, with carbon dates of close to 4,000 years ago. There was also on the surface of the cairn a well-made and intact inverted food vessel. The larger cist was sunk in a pit that had two small cup marked stones and a saddle quern set into its edge. Another possible cup mark was found on the edge of the cist capstone. Cremated bone of more than one individual was found in the soil under the cover. In a dark layer below that was a food vessel on its side. Further down was dark earth with flint flakes and beads. The second cist was particularly well made from a compact, shiny stone quarried from a nearby hillside; it contained several separate cremations, probably in bags, sealed in with a flat capstone. It seems that when a second kerb wall was added to the cairn a platform or entrance may have been an access to it.

A 'Food vessel containing the cremated remains of a child, found at the top of the cairn as a later insertion.

Part of the cairn had been ploughed into, as sharp cuts in some of the stones showed. Two complete rigs and furrows were excavated, and there was an earlier plough soil under the cairn kerbs. Mixed with the plough soil were very small pieces of Bronze Age pottery made locally.

The number of early Bronze Age 'food vessels' in the Cheviots shot up during these excavations, and Beaker pottery was to be added at another dig on Wether Hill. Interesting though these artefacts are, a major objective of these excavations was to find more about how people farmed and lived; the finding of two such important burial cairns was unexpected, and they had to be explored thoroughly as part of the landscape. It gives the media a good story, and arouses public interest, but there are objectives that lead often to no artefacts or significant structures, and this kind of excavation can be hard and frustrating work.

Closer to the village, at Ingram South, on a platform behind the village hall, a site revealed from the air by parch marks was a buried pre-Roman or Romano-British enclosure, which when selectively excavated, showed that barley had been stored and processed there. Carbon dating showed that this had taken place in AD 150.

No excavation had been arranged before to look at the fields themselves, and this was the next task of the project, beginning with the terraces that we walk over when we make the ascent from the car park to the top of Brough Law. Terraces are one answer to the difficulty of ploughing on a steep slope and for the retention of moisture, and the practice is still wide spread in the world. In the Ingram valley the systems are fossilised, and some of the horizontal walls and small fields are crossed by wide, curving rig and furrow systems that follow the hill slopes down. The contrast between the two systems makes them easy to pick out but they had not been dug or dated. With the discovery of evidence of earlier groups of people using the landscape, and the certainty that there are many visible Iron Age and Romano-British settlements, it is possible that fields may have been set out in pre-Roman times and continued to be used by later people. This is more obvious in lowland areas, where many early field systems appear in dry conditions from the air. The project over two seasons put very long trenches through terraces below Brough Law and close to two enclosures recently cleared from forest. Beginning with two small-scale explorations, it soon became apparent that the walls of some of the terraces were of monumental proportions, with massive pyroclast boulders incorporated, equal to those used to make the tri-radial cairn on Turf Knowe. Other walls were made of smaller stuff. A very deep trench was dug through the fields, and the underlying geology consisting of thick deposits of water- and ice-washed sediments was revealed.

In all, three terraces were trenched; the walls were not built until plough soil had accumulated, so the walls were built to prevent the soil from slipping downhill.

It is clear from the air that many small Romano-British farmsteads survive, surrounded by field systems that do not have to be contemporary with them. A site called Little Haystacks was chosen for excavation; it had a long boundary wall beside it and field systems around. Underneath the site excavation revealed a palisaded (fenced) enclosure of an older settlement and there were two pits of

Excavation of terraces where grain was grown since prehistoric times.

c. 1000 BC. The boundary wall's construction was well defined, but the enclosure itself contained very few artefacts in its disturbed interior. The radio -carbon date from under the boundary wall was early medieval. It was not possible to date the field systems adjoining it—a timely reminder that although excavation is essential, it does not answer all our questions.

A separate group of archaeologists with a strong voluntary membership ran a separate but related dig at Wether Hill. The hill has a large and complex series of ringworks and house sites and a cross ridge dyke. The Northumberland Archaeology Group meticulously surveyed this before choosing key areas to excavate, and began work on a piece of grassland that had only a grassed cairn visible. The cairn proved to have had its centre dug out, but a main feature was the addition of an outer kerb some distance away from the original edge. More importantly, a grassy area, which showed nothing on the surface, covered a number of curved trenches for fences, marked by slots and small upright stones to take the thin timbers. These enclosures had been truncated by later ploughing, but one contained the ring-groove foundations of a wooden building. It became clearer as the area of excavation was extended was that there were enclosures of different times in the Iron Age containing buildings. More dramatically, a much earlier pit was excavated that was timber-lined like a coffin to contain early Bronze Age burials.

The survey of this area was extensive, taking ten years, in which layers of time were revealed and the finds intelligently displayed, much of them in the National Park's Ingram centre. All the sites have been written up and published. Since this

Kirknewton in Glendale.

investigation of 'one of England's most extraordinary yet little investigated archae-ology landscapes' (Paul Frodsham), other emphases have now shifted to other parts of the county.

GLENDALE

The River Bowmont changes its name to Glen (after the Welsh *glyn*, a valley) where it is joined by the College Burn near Kirknewton. It flows towards the Milfield Plain to meet the River Till, a tributary of the River Tweed. The College, Bowmont and Glen valleys provide restricted but fertile agricultural land, but we see again the use of hillslopes for cultivation terraces. The Glen skirts the steep edge of the volcanic rocks of the Cheviots, and the towering hills follow a curve towards Wooler, their summits overlooking the large dried-up glacial lake with its rich agricultural sands, clays and gravels, flanked by the sandstone ridges and coastal plain.

Wooler is the only town of any size, lying as its name implies at the edge of the Wooler Water, its eighteenth- and nineteenth-century houses set on a hillside with extensive views. There is a 'Tenter Hill' leading from the A697 where cloth used to be stretched on frames, a reminder of what we mean when we say that we are on tenterhooks. There are some friendly pubs, shops, bank, car parks and churches. There used to be a defensive tower, described in 1541 as 'a marvellous convenient place for the defence of the country thereabout'. It is a pleasant town with a stable population, known as a gateway for the exploration of the Cheviot Hills and for the swathe of interesting country in other directions. Caravan sites have spread along the main road where the English army camped at the haugh before moving on to do battle with the Scottish army in 1513. At Homildon Hill, below the Cheviots, on the way to Coldstream from Wooler is the site of a lesser battle in 1402 between the old enemies Percy and Douglas, traditionally marked by a standing stone to the east of the road that in fact marks the site of a prehistoric burial. Shakespeare begins the first part of *Henry IV* with this battle where the protagonists 'did spend a sad and bloody hour', making Hotspur's refusal to surrender his prisoners to the king a bone of contention that was to lead to Hotspur's death. A large Scots army reached as far as Newcastle and was returning with plunder to the fording places on the Tweed when they were ambushed. One vital factor in the defeat of the Scots was the use of Welsh archers, and the battle became a rout in which hundreds were drowned in the Tweed or the Till.

High above this site is Humbleton Hill, probably meaning that it was 'bare-headed', in that the vegetation had been cut off; it has a large prehistoric enclosure. The National Park Authority is making an intensive survey of all the forts in its area, *Discovering our Hillfort Heritage*, and has made management agreements with landowners so that people can visit some of them. To our great advantage, they have also produced a number of leaflets that illustrate what is to be seen and how to reach them, including Humbleton and Yeavering.

Humbleton is one of the strongest forts, with circular hut floors cut into platforms

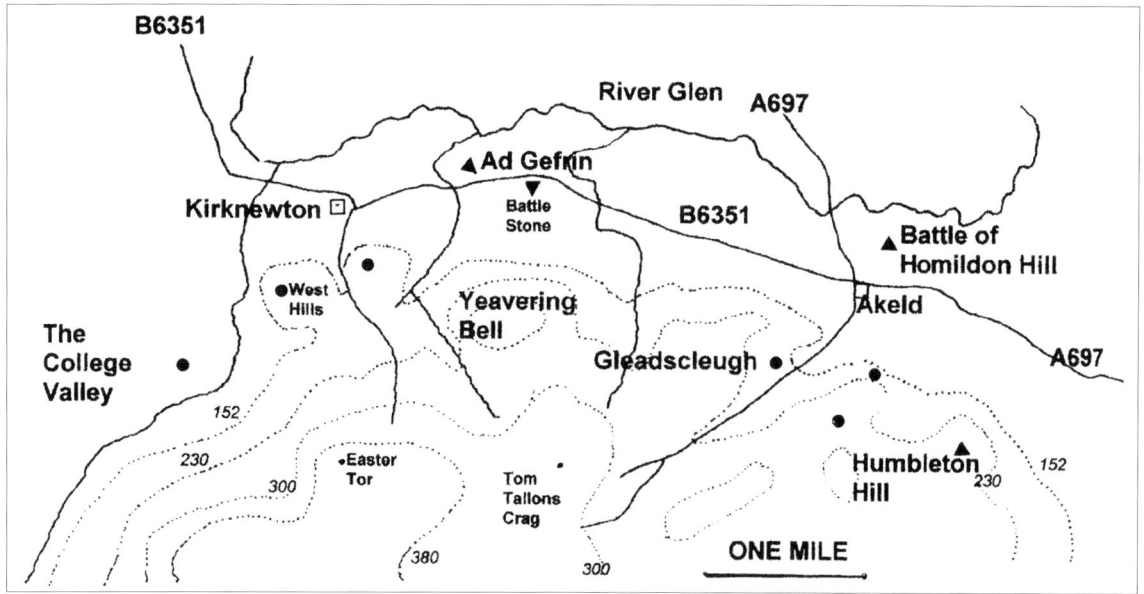

A sketch map of the north-east Cheviots and Glendale.

Humbleton Hill to Monday Cleugh.

that overlook a ravine. It is centred on the summit surrounded by a massive stone wall, containing hut platforms, to which a later transverse wall was added. It has a much larger enclosure outside this, but as an excavation at Dod Law across the valley proved that the outer wall of a fort is not necessarily a later addition, the same may apply here. Only excavation would prove that. Lack of any real archaeological detail should not prevent us from reacting to a site like this, and I offer this poem:

High Humbleton

High Humbleton, bare-headed hill, with half-closed eyes
Takes in pale shadow shapes
That flit across the valley's furrowed flatlands
Among flecked feeding gulls, scorning this idle game
Devised by sun and clouds.

A hill fort tonsure of grey rock tumbles to its neck
And bears indignity of hikers' cairn heaped on its head,
Shoulders hunched against the cold.
Its ancient body crinkles into unknown depths
From which he rose from molten rock,
Roaring defiance, blacking sun
Until the hissing chaos of his pent-up anger ceased.

Margin of ice-scoured, rounded, clustered hills
With tree-strewn cleughs
Focused on flat-topped Cheviot;
This hill an eastern sentinel.

Bracken's copper, laced with bright green winter grass
From summer's feet and narrow tread of sheep,
 Spreads like a rash.
Heather, tight in clusters, raises dust
In raked mid-winter sun
To mark the passage of a badger or a fox.
There is a stillness that no life can shake,
No re-arrangement of the sun-tossed clouds
Can penetrate the surface of the hills.
Below the scanty soil are vesicles of blown-out gas
Replugged with shining minerals in rich red rock,
Forever hard and cold.

A lingering light upon cold hills and sunward slopes
Coaxes a story thousands of seasons long.

Barrows for the dead, like crusted pimples
Break the sloping ground,
And cord rig combs the hillside, once a bed of grain,
Scarcely a mouthful now for sullen sheep.
Faint hollow ways and intermittent walls
Grow and fade with moving light.
Shallow pits of shadows speak
Of houses in enclosures platform-perched
Or huddled round the hill fort's top.
These soils are wasted now.
Only deep-set lynchets or the massive hill fort walls stand proud.
Only a patient eye can now detect
The traces of the face beneath the veil,
And Humbleton has seen it all.
When moonrise mists the valleys with its eerie light
The dark mass broods and gathers to itself
So many lives, so many times.

The borders of the hills curve round to flank the River Glen at Akeld, where another Iron Age promontory fort at Gleadscleugh makes use of a strategic position for defence and for the siting of round timber houses set into scoops on the slopes. The Glen valley road gives a lovely view of the hill country, with a narrow road leading off to the College Valley, accessible on foot from a car park at Hethpool at the north end. For those who can climb the hills, the best view is from Great Hetha, another hill fort that looks down on a smaller version, Little Hetha. The remains of a large stone circle and approach stones lie at the foot of the valley. Prehistoric and Romano-British sites are visible everywhere, and there is an especially important system of lynchets similar to those in the Ingram Valley.

In the main valley, Kirknewton is a small village with a small school that has recently survived attempts to close it. The church of St Gregory the Great is striking from the outside, for its tall nineteenth-century tower is built from a variety of coloured stones from quarry, river bed and field clearance, and includes a piece of medieval grave slab. Below it is the grave of the great social reformer, Josephine Butler. In another lifetime we have the graves of young airmen stationed locally who were killed in the Second World War. Today only gliders use the airstrips. The church itself, though much restored, is based on pointed tunnel vaults in the south transept and chancel; they are very strong and rugged, as befits anything built in this perilous Border area. Another survival of the past is a piece of twelfth-century sculpture set into an east wall. Known locally as 'The Kilted Magi', the skirts that the three kings are wearing as they bring their gifts to the young Christ and his mother are traditional medieval wear for men.

Although the contribution of Josephine Butler to our modern history is considerable, the area is perhaps better known for the site of Yeavering. Really there are

The Kilted Magi.

Yeavering Bell.

two Yeaverings: the largest hill fort in the north, and the valley settlement below it.

Yeavering Bell has been made easily accessible to walkers. The name *Ad Gefrin* means 'of the wild goats', and the climb to the summit gives you a good chance of seeing some. At the top there is a massive wall that circles the summit for 950 m, enclosing about 13.5 acres (5.5 h). Originally its base was 10 feet (3 m) thick, and stones quarried from the hillside and top were tapered upwards. Now they have collapsed and spread outwards, in places up to *c.* 26 feet (8 m) wide. This wall encloses scoops in the ground and flat platforms on which about 130 wooden huts were built. Some of them had ring grooves into which upright timbers were slotted. Roofs would have been thatched with heather or straw. An example of a reconstructed stone roundhouse can be seen at Brigantium, Rochester, Redesdale. What always strikes me when I climb to the top is how people could have lived there for any length of time, for even in summer it can be cold and windswept. May we assume a different climate 2,500 years ago?

The effort to reach the top is well worth it, for the views (in a county of magnificent views) take in an enormous range of country to the sea and across the Tweed.

In 1862 the local historian George Tate wrote:

> Few places in Northumberland have attracted more attention than Yeavering Bell . . . Every tourist and pleasure seeker, who rambles along the Borders, must climb to its summit, pore over its mysterious monuments and enjoy the extensive and rich view it commands.

The importance of the Milfield Plain is clear, a level area where henges, rows of posts and routeways have been revealed. The Coupland 'henge', a large cattle enclosure, is claimed by Clive Waddington to be the oldest henge-type construction in Britain, *The Maelmin Heritage Trail* includes a reconstruction of the Milfield North henge. The sandstone scarps that fringe the plain at Dod Law, Doddington North Moor, and Broomridge do not seem imposing from here. The best time to see this view is on a fine summer's evening, when low light rakes the landscape to reveal all the subtle indentations that make geology and history so interesting.

From the hill a plateau can clearly be seen above the Glen that is the site of the Anglo-Saxon settlement of Ad Gefrin. Found from the air in 1949, there were no standing structures visible, but outlined as parch marks were the trenches of timbers that proved to be the palace and other buildings of King Edwin. As his main power base was at Bamburgh, the choice of Yeavering as a secondary one was because there was an important part of his kingdom here. Long before, prehistoric activity began in the valley; burials, a henge and standing stone, known as the *Battle Stone*, standing *c.* 10 feet (3 m) tall and re-erected in 1924, are a part of the life and ritual here. The presence of the hill fort confirms its importance, on the scale of a capital city. The quietness of the site today and the fact that there is nothing to see shows how power bases move. It was established in the seventh-century and was subject to raids, re-building and destruction until the decision was made to move it to Maelmin on the Milfield Plain. Its life and death are tied to King Edwin's. He presided over warriors and administrators who lived around him, and based their fortunes on service to him. His influence and power were wide-ranging, and his success would keep the stream of warriors coming to him, for their reward was money, preference, fame and land. Without them he was nothing, but the whole hierarchy depended on the peasants who had the job of raising food and paying their rulers. It is the old, old story, repeated endlessly. One assumes that the land at that time was capable of supporting people of ambition

The early site was a stockade with small rectangular cottages. Then in the mid-seventh century a great hall was built of squared timbers set vertically in trenches. Another important and unusual building was a kind of theatre, a semi-circular arrangement of seats in tiers, focusing into a point at a dais, which Edwin had extended to seat 300 people. This and the hall have so much to say about society and power, for the king travelled with his attendants, lived in the hall with them and possibly gave judgements from the dais. With him he brought Bishop Paulinus, reputed to have converted him to Christianity and to have been his chief adviser from AD 626–33. Probably the 'church' moved around with the king and his retinue, and to Paulinus are attributed many baptisms, some perhaps in the river Glen. Edwin was killed at Hatfield by Cadwallon and Penda in AD 633. His successor Oswald became king, defeated Cadwallon somewhere near Hexham and encouraged Scottish priests to come to Lindisfarne where the monastery was modelled on Iona. Oswald was to become the first royal Northumbrian martyr and saint.

The Milfield Plain from Yeavering Bell.

Power clearly rested on military might, but ideas too were potent. When Edwin was being persuaded to turn to Christ, Bede records that one argument that counted heavily was the vision of our mortality. As we picture that big timber hall below the Cheviot hill fort, we can see the walls flickering with firelight from a large central fire. The king and his men are there, eating and enjoying each other's fellowship. Outside it is dark, cold and windy, and the darkness holds uncertainty. Suddenly a sparrow flies in, takes in the scene for a moment, a little bewildered perhaps and a little afraid, then flies out again. Life is like that; uncertainty about where we come from and where we go after death, but for a while we may have a little warmth and company.

Finale
The Return of the Lindisfarne Gospels

An event well worthy of celebration has been the creation of the Lindisfarne Gospels, a great survival of the early Church crusade to place the Gospels at the centre of what was to be for many a new religion. That this book has actually survived is miraculous, considering Viking invasion and destruction of monasteries, its being carried for years along with the body of Saint Cuthbert until it found with him a home at what is now Durham cathedral , but later looted by Henry VIII's men and taken to London. The return of the book to Durham in 2013, whether temporarily or permanently, has been applauded by many in the north to such an extent that the perusal of one page in its 'home' has become a visit of great significance to them. There is a more accessible replica, not of such iconic status, that many others saw when it went on tour in Northumberland. That the original script was the work of one man, and the binding and cover the work of other monks, is remarkable when one considers of the low-light condition under which it was written. It also required hundreds of calf-skins to make the pages. The motivation for the effort and skill that inspired it was that the word of God needed to be presented to the world with the best work that men could achieve.

The establishment of Christianity in the North was a mixture of force, conviction and display of its power in opposition to Anglo-Saxon paganism. We know about this struggle from the Venerable Bede of Jarrow who gathered together all the information that he could from visitors about the history of the Church, without straying too far from Jarrow monastery, where he collected his great store of information and gave much in return. His account concentrated on episodes in the early life of the Church, particularly stressing miracles that confirmed its power. This is not surprising, for one way in which the new Church could combat paganism was to show that its 'magic' was stronger. The pioneers were also encouraged not just to destroy paganism, but to use its sacred sites for the building of wooden churches and the erection of crosses.

Monks were trained to go among the Anglo-Saxons to convert them, and as Christianity took root and grew, so did their churches, which in some cases held relics, displayed beauty, and were unlike the houses where people lived. Art played a

Some pages from the
Lindisfarne Gospels

crucial part in in the production of books, copied and illustrated by hand, either for use here or abroad. Although wood was the main building material at this time, stone was to replace it eventually for the most important buildings. In Northumberland shaped Roman stone was plentiful in the Wall zone, but masons had to be brought from the Continent to re-introduce the lost art of making mortar. About 30 per cent of Northumberland medieval churches have some Saxon features. They were modified when fashions in building changed and now are multi-period. For example, the Norman Conquest was determined to impose its dominance on the population, and their building styles for churches and castles demonstrate this. The survivals the late Saxon period are some tall, unbuttressed towers, long naves, apsidal east ends and high round-topped windows, with concentrations in the Tyne Valley from Warden eastwards, and outstanding examples such as Whittingham further north.

Hexham has the remarkable survival of a Saxon crypt, built at the time of Wilfrid, and survives along with documents that describe the interiors of some of these buildings. The monasteries led the way in design, yet one of the most important settlements of all, Lindisfarne, must have been built over after the Anglo-Saxon period. The monastic settlement there may still be buried, but it was a church among small stone or wooden huts.

The two great forces in early Christianity were the Celtic and the Roman before the Synod of Whitby decided that the latter was to prevail. This decision linked Britain with Europe, making it part of 'the universal Catholic Church'.

The impetus for evangelism came from some outstanding figures such as Aidan and Cuthbert and other monks, but the support of secular kings was essential to the growth of the Church, for their wealth and fighting ability fostered and protected it.

Holy Island, originally called Lindisfarrne, was one of the most important centres of Christianity in the world before it was shattered by Viking raiders, which caused the monks to carry Cuthbert's body and prized objects such as The Gospels with it for many miles and years until it found rest in Durham. With the Norman Conquest, the Church became dominated by an aristocracy which showed its power and dominance building fine churches and castles that echoed its power bases on the Continent.

Today the writing of the Lindisfarne Gospels is celebrated in the north-east now that the original has been loaned by London for display in Durham Cathedral, but the quality of the work had been recognised throughout the Christian world. However, the Gospels are not just a skilful and extravagant art form, but are the way in which the message of Christianity was brought to all people. The crucial thing is why they were written.

The summer of 2013 witnessed pilgrimage of about 2,000 people to Lindisfarne, and in a united act of worship people of many religions gathered in friendship to celebrate what the Gospels stand for.

Whittingham Saxon tower before the top was blown off.

Hexham crypt.

CELEBRATING NORTHUMBERLAND'S HISTORY

A cause for celebration in recent years has been the interest in discovering more about the county's past in literature, music, research into original sources and their preservation, and in the amount of archaeological work that has been carried out. In the latter case much of the county has been surveyed from the air, revealing many hitherto unknown sites, especially with the help of non-professional and independent archaeologists who have been trained by professionals.

The discoveries made and recorded may be of single objects, such as a Romano-British statue of Hercules found at the junction of the rivers North and South Tyne found many years ago but only now brought out of storage and erected in Acomb village, Hexham.

Projects such as the thorough excavation of multi-period sites on the Milfield plain and in the Cheviot Hills around Ingram, the rescue of many crumbling prehistoric sites along the coast, thorough surveys on many sites found recently, the recording of all prehistoric rock art and its entry on the Internet with its 17 million 'hits' world-wide; the detailed recording of buildings and assessment of what needs to be done to preserve them are all causes for celebration, as it means that public and private bodies take their history seriously.

THE ROMAN WALL CORRIDOR

The wall has always been an attraction, even to the extent of taking resources away from other periods and places. Now declared a World Heritage site and having its own cross-country walk, it is even more popular and attracts thousands of people each year to visit and walk it. It has to be constantly maintained, and more of its story is revealed by excavation. At Vindolanda, which runs itself as a Trust, we have one of the most exciting archaeological programmes in the world, particularly with the discovery of large amounts of Roman material culture and of the 'writing tablets' which give a unique insight into life on the Wall zone. In the central section the scenery is awe-inspiring, and places like Housesteads fort offer not only much of the plan of a fort, but marvellous views all around. Recently there was a string of beacons lighted along the Wall, which brought in more visitors from all over the world.

Now there is a plan to build a large centre at Twice Brewed where English Heritage and the National Park can attract even more visitors.

OTHER PROJECTS

This is not the place to list all the projects that are opening up more of Northumberland to the world, but there are many on different scales such as churches trying to raise money to repair ancient buildings, such as the Saxon tower at Warden, or buildings connected with the old lead mining industries of the Pennines.

A Romano-British Hercules, found in Tynedale.

The Roman wall: one of the finest views of the middle section. (*Tony Iley*)

In Hexhamshire the Dukesfield smelter's toxic fumes are carried over a constructed 'gothic' bridge. The site is currently being excavated.

A possible change in the fortunes of the area that still bears minerals is that there is a need for zinc extraction, and the old lead mining areas around Allendale are being investigated to see whether this can be mined in depth, and already there is talk of 500 jobs that may result from such a scheme. After the lead mines closed, British Steel used feldspar from this area for their blast furnaces. People need jobs.

One of the most ambitious projects is at Hexham, Abbey, where the buildings that were taken over by the Lord of the Manor after the Dissolution of the Monasteries have been restored to Abbey use. As well as being the town parish church, the Abbey is a main attraction in the town, including pilgrims, and to use the buildings to display the history of the town, to provide working areas for school parties and others, and to provide another space for the townspeople is the aim.

Seaton Delaval Hall has been renovated and re-opened. Alnwick Castle Gardens continue to develop—and so it goes on.

One particularly-pleasing commemoration has been the 500th anniversary of the Battle of Flodden (9 September 1513), with an absence of 're-enactments' that seem to glorify battle. Instead, there were serious services that recognised the horror of that episode and concentrated on reconciliation.

Northumberland has something for everyone, and its geology has conspired to give a superb coastline, traffic-free areas like hills and scarps where people can breathe, lovely rivers, so many viewpoints, well-controlled agriculture and evidence of a past that includes the industries that built modern Britain. Those who think of it as an industrial wasteland, especially a misguided peer stated recently in the House of Lords, have never visited it, sad to say for them.

Further Reading

One of the most useful reference books is *The Buildings of England: Northumberland* by Nikolaus Pevsner and Ian Richmond. The second edition is revised by John Grundy, Grace McCombie, Peter Ryder and Humphrey Welfare (1992) Penguin Books.

Northumberland County History Committee (1893) *History of Northumberland*. This 15-volume work is still one of the most important sources.

Articles in local journals such as the old-established *Archaeologia Aeliana* (The Society of Antiquaries of Newcastle-upon-Tyne) the more recent *Northern Archaeology* (Northumberland Archaeology Group), and the County Council's annual Archaeology in Northumberland, provide up-dates of research and excavations.

The National Trust, Northumberland National Park, English Heritage, The Vindolanda Trust, and independent publications found in churches and information centres have publications to suit most needs. Local History Societies have their own publications, notably the Association of Northumberland Local History Societies and the Hexham Local History Society's *Hexham Historian*. Local Library services will provide further information, and standard works on various aspects of Northumberland's history and landscape have important Bibliographies. There is a large number of publications of research into most aspects of county history.

Among popular guides for visitors are those on guided walks.

Books by Stan Beckensall specifically on Northumberland:

1993. *Hexham: history beneath our feet* (Hexham, Robson)
1993. *The Spindlestone Dragon* (The Abbey Press, Hexham playscript)
1994. *Life and Death in Prehistoric Northumberland* (Butler Publishing)
2001. *Prehistoric Rock Art in Northumberland* (Tempus, Stroud)
2003. *Prehistoric Northumberland* (Tempus)

2004. *Northumberland Place Names* (Butler)

2004. *Northumberland: Shadows of the Past* (Tempus)

2006. *Place Names and Field Names of Northumberland* (Tempus)

2007. *Hexham: History and Guide* (Tempus)

2008. *Unquiet Grave: a novel for young people* (Powdene, Newcastle)

2008. *Northumberland from the air* (History Press, Stroud)

2010. *Empire Halts Here: Viewing the Heart of Hadrian's Wall* (Amberley, Stroud)

2010. *Northumberland Viewpoints* (Amberley)

2010. *Northumberland's Coastal Castles* (Amberley)

2012. *Northumberland Hills and Valleys* (Amberley)

2012. *Hexham Through Time* (Amberley)

2013. *Northumberland Churches* (Amberley)

2014. *Prehistoric Rock Art in Northumberland*

2014. *Pilgrimage: A Tour of Northumberland in Pictures and Poems* (Fonthill Media)

The above books contain useful references to other books on Northumberland.

Index